The Elusive State of Jefferson

OTHER BOOKS BY PETER LAUFER

No Animals Were Harmed
Forbidden Creatures
The Dangerous World of Butterflies
Slow News
Calexico
Neon Nevada (with Sheila Swan Laufer)
Hope Is a Tattered Flag (with Markos Kounalakis)
Mission Rejected
Wetback Nation
Exodus to Berlin
Highlights of a Lowlife (editor)
Shock and Awe
Made in Mexico (illustrated by Susan L. Roth)
Wireless Etiquette
Safety and Security for Women Who Travel (with Sheila Swan Laufer)
Inside Talk Radio
A Question of Consent
When Hollywood Was Fun (with Gene Lester)
Nightmare Abroad
Iron Curtain Rising

The
Elusive State
of Jefferson

A Journey through
the 51st State

PETER LAUFER, PhD

TWODOT®

GUILFORD, CONNECTICUT
HELENA, MONTANA
AN IMPRINT OF GLOBE PEQUOT PRESS

A · TWODOT® · BOOK

TwoDot is an imprint of Globe Pequot Press and a registered trademark of
Morris Book Publishing, LLC.

All photographs by author unless otherwise indicated

Project Editor: Tracee Williams
Layout: Sue Murray
Map by Melissa Baker © Morris Book Publishing, LLC

Library of Congress Cataloging-in-Publication Data

Laufer, Peter.
The elusive state of Jefferson : a personal journey through the 51st
state / Peter Laufer, PhD. —First edition.
pages cm
Includes bibliographical references and index.
ISBN 978-0-7627-8836-1
1. California, Northern—Politics and government. 2. Oregon—Politics
and government. 3. Statehood (American politics) 4. California,
Northern—Description and travel. 5. Oregon—Description and travel. 6.
Environmentalism—California, Northern. 7. California, Northern—Social
conditions. 8. Oregon—History—20th century. 9. California,
Northern—History—20th century. I. Title.
F867.5.L38 2013
979.4'053—dc23
2013015002

Printed in the United States of America

10 9 8 7 6 5 4 3 2 1

For Sheila, as always,
with love for putting me in such a state

All we ask is to be left alone.

—*Jefferson Davis, from his Inaugural Address as*
president of the Confederacy, 1861

I want to be alone.
—*Greta Garbo, playing Grusinskaya in the film* Grand Hotel, *1932*

This is not the last of it.

—*General Jefferson Columbus Davis,*
moments prior to shooting his superior officer, 1862

The sheep are happier of themselves, than under the care of wolves.

—*Thomas Jefferson, in a 1787 letter*
to William Stevens Smith

Contents

Contents

What Is Jefferson?

AFTER THE 2012 PRESIDENTIAL ELECTION, HUNDREDS OF THOUSANDS of Americans from all fifty states signed secession petitions, setting off a flurry of media declarations that a "neo-secessionist movement" was underway. Because such movements have come and gone throughout the history of this country, I wonder if the desire to break from the pack, to redraw lines, to question our allegiances, is somehow hardwired in the American mind. No matter how we espouse the virtues of working together to build better communities, we can't quite shake our identities as rugged individualists.

Nowhere has this urge for independence played out more plainly than in Oregon—a land of Don Berry's *Trask* and Ken Kesey's *Sometimes a Great Notion;* a birthplace of direct democracy and urban growth boundaries; a place where moderate Republicanism thrived long before and after such across-the-aisle efforts were considered heroic; a geography of immense production and potential, richly festooned in a thousand shades of green to the west and a thousand shades of brown to the east. This combination of natural capital, independence, and idealism have made Oregon a stronghold in secessionist imaginings, including Ernest Callenbach's Ecotopia, David McCloskey's Cascadia, and the State of Jefferson, richly detailed in these pages by Peter Laufer, a journalist who has been fascinated by the borders and boundaries that separate and unite people.

It's no surprise that land and resources are the backdrop against which the dramas and dreams of Jeffersonians play out. Perhaps we learn best about ourselves and one another in the context of places that inspire in us a sense of loyalty and belonging, whether towering redwoods or rivers speckled with salmon and gold. These are the places that we fight over and live for. These are the places that come to represent our ideas of how we should live and who we should be. We've had these conversations for decades in saloons and parlors, on streets and in courtrooms, in books and newspapers and, more recently, through online forums that connect us across time and space, while driving us farther away from those with whom we don't see eye to eye.

Laufer's journey through Jefferson takes us both across and into the borderlands in question, but also—through history, stories, legends, and science—into the ideas that residents of the region continue to grapple with. These always-inspiring and sometimes-infuriating citizens of Jefferson have little use for the municipalities that mean to tell them who they are and to whom they belong. Instead, they carry with them a notion, at once troubling and comforting, that they are tribes of their own making and that the geopolitical lines on a map won't deter them from imagining something different.

The question we are left with after hearing their stories and struggles is an eternal one, one that we might ask everyday as citizens of this real and imagined place called America: How can we learn to live well alone and together?

Kathleen Holt
Oregon Humanities communications director and
editor of Oregon Humanities *magazine*
Portland, 2013

Where Is Jefferson?

At seven years old, my son Leo became devoted to the State of Jefferson. I don't think he cared much about the argument that Sacramento and Salem represented big government infringing on the freedoms of others. And I don't even think he gave much thought to the coho salmon or spotted owl. Rather it was a sixteen-inch rainbow trout pulling on his line that made him dig his heels into the mud on the bank of the Upper Sacramento River just north of Dunsmuir. It was at that moment, with crystal clear waters below and beautiful pines above, that my son fell in love with what some people call the State of Jefferson.

As a number of people interviewed in this book have said, the State of Jefferson is more than a place; it is an idea, an idea rooted in the complicated, sometimes inspiring and other times painful history of our country. The idea of Jefferson plays itself out in northern California and southern Oregon with a seriousness and sometimes playfulness that we can learn from.

So what is the idea of Jefferson? Is the state of Jefferson, as one person says, "a benign fairy tale," or is it a "petri dish example of a devolving American dream," or is it something else completely? Even the name itself raises questions about the character of the region. Some say it was named after Thomas Jefferson, the third president of the United States, others say Jefferson Davis, the president of the Confederacy, and still others consider the victorious Jefferson C. Davis, the US general in the Modoc War, a candidate.

Let's assume it was named after Thomas Jefferson, a president who has been called the "American Sphinx" because of the contradictions and inconsistencies that have created some ambiguity in his thoughts, intentions, and the historical impact of his ideas and policies. He was the author of the Declaration of Independence and yet he enslaved people; he is a fascination for biographers, historians, and the public and his writings take up twelve volumes. Yet he only gave two public speeches while president. Most notoriously, Jefferson is considered by many to have been an advocate of small central government, while, in fact, he hugely expanded federal territory with the Louisiana Purchase and increased the federal government's war power with an expanded navy. So how is it that the northernmost portion of California and the southern part of Oregon felt so akin to our third president to name a place after him?

Peter Laufer dives into the State of Jefferson, shares beers, laughs and serious talk with those who live there, grappling with the meaning of their special corner of the world. Along the way, Laufer uncovers a wonderful small town trust, along with one of the most surprising media stories of the last century, while he enjoys a similar love of the place that my son Leo discovered for himself on the banks of the Upper Sacramento River.

Ralph Lewin
President and Chief Executive Officer
California Council for the Humanities
San Francisco, 2013

Preface

Here I sit in my library just a short bicycle ride from the campus of the University of Oregon, where I teach. Eugene is bisected from its twin city Springfield by the sparkling and meandering Willamette River. Reputation separates the cities, too. Springfield, with its downtown known for seedy strip bars and empty storefronts, fights the image of a down-on-its-luck blue-collar dead end. The lumber mills are quiet, the railroad spurs empty. Across the river, Eugene tries to shake off the sixties and its lingering fame as a counterculture mecca for urbanites seeking an enclave of hipsters far from big city bustle. This dichotomy is well expressed by local jokes.

Some target Springfield. Question: Why do people in Eugene ride bicycles? Answer: For the exercise, to save gas, and to reduce pollution. Question: And why do people in Springfield ride bicycles? Answer: Because they lost their drivers' licenses after getting too many DUIs. The disparaging term for Springfield in some Eugene circles is Springtucky.

Others target Eugene, of course. Question: Why did the hippie move to Eugene? Answer: Because he heard there were no jobs available there.

───

We all seek borders. Most of us want to surround ourselves with the familiar and with people who share our philosophies. It's easy to feel as if those who are not familiar and who do not share our philosophies dismiss our needs and desires. It's easy to fear them as the Other. Borders can provide us with both a real and imagined sense of security—but always only temporarily. The Great Wall of China is a tourist attraction and the Berlin Wall is an eradicated vague memory.

Years ago I lived in Silver City, Nevada, one of the Gold and Silver Rush boomtowns of the mid-1800s. Just four miles up the road was the more famous Virginia City, where Samuel L. Clemens renamed himself Mark Twain when he took a job writing for the *Territorial Enterprise*. Later he recounted his adventures at the newspaper in *Roughing It* with words all journalists should take to heart: "As I grew better acquainted with the business and learned the run of the sources of information I ceased to require the aid of fancy to any large extent, and became able to fill my columns without diverging noticeably from the domain of fact." A little over a hundred years later I found myself editor of what was a competing newspaper to Twain's, the *Gold Hill News*. We brought the *News* back to life after a ninety-two-year hiatus, a lapse we noted in a sardonic front page box that apologized for any inconvenience to subscribers.

Virginia City was known as the Queen of the Comstock. The Comstock Lode—which ran from Virginia City down to Gold Hill and on to Silver City, Dayton, and out to Sutro—provided the North with riches it needed to fight the Civil War (the war, of course, that kept the Confederacy from successfully seceding). Nevada became a state in 1864, at a time when President Lincoln needed its pro-Union support. Hence Nevada's state motto: Battle Born. By the time I moved to Silver, Virginia City's main drag, C Street, was reduced to an ersatz Disneyland. The Delta Saloon was offering fake newspapers for sale with "Your Name in Headlines!" A photo studio made sepia souvenir portraits and provided Old West costumes to those of its customers seeking authenticity. The wooden sidewalks of C Street were littered with the requisite number of ice cream parlors and T-shirt shops assigned to such tourist traps.

Those four miles separating us in Silver City from them in Virginia City were endless. Silver's population peaked during the boom years at about ten thousand. There were 150 of us in town when I was in residence. We were urban refugees—not unlike the city folks who moved to Eugene in the sixties—seeking a respite from the hustle of the city. We mixed with the few locals from the mining days who had stayed on in Silver as the boomtown dwindled into ghost town status.

But it wasn't just the honky-tonk tourist hustlers versus back-to-the-land types that separated us from our neighbors up the hill. Virginia City is the county seat of Storey County. The county line is on the north side of Silver City. We lived in Lyon County and were governed by the county commissioners in Yerington, sixty-three miles southeast of us (unless we shaved a few miles off the drive by taking the Weeks Cutoff past Silver Springs, a dirt road). We felt ignored and neglected by the county government and considered ourselves treated as if we were an ugly stepsister dismissed by the power brokers as well past her prime and easy to forget. Yet we harbored zero interest in aligning ourselves with the predatory merchant class in Virginia City that controlled Storey County and defined its alien culture.

Enforcing an existing social and political union that brings together divergent types can be difficult at best, disastrous at worst. The breakup of Yugoslavia in the 1990s is an example, that relatively recent balkanization of the Balkans. In the autumn of 1990 I was traveling through Yugoslavia and met an ultranationalist Serbian fellow distributing propaganda on the streets of Belgrade. "Serbians in Croatia," he preached at me, "they haven't got their rights there."

The next year Croatia seceded from Yugoslavia. Serbs attacked, and the war between the two lasted over three years before Croatia, its economy devastated, prevailed and established its sovereignty.

When I worked as an NBC News correspondent, I was assigned to the network's Washington, DC bureau. My family and I lived across the District Line in Maryland. Our congressman and our senators represented us in Washington. No such luck for many of my colleagues who chose to live closer to the bureau's DC studios. Congress governs the District of Columbia. It allows some aspects of the city's day-to-day life to be controlled by the DC city government, but home rule is limited. And Congress retains the ultimate authority over the District; it can (and does) change the status of home rule when it sees fit. Despite this authority the Feds maintain over the city, Washingtonians enjoy no vote up on Capitol Hill. The District is allowed to send a delegate to the House, a delegate who can suggest and debate legislation, but not vote. District citizens are barred from any role in the Senate.

Yet those who dwell in the District must pay federal income taxes. Hence the popular local license plate legend, TAXATION WITHOUT REPRESENTATION. Taxation without representation is of course what led to the Boston Tea Party in 1773, a precursor to our American Revolution—which was secession from the Mother Country.

My wife, Sheila, periodically muses about splitting California into two states, a north and a south. She's a native of our Golden State, born and raised in Oakland, an Oak-town girl who moved just a few miles north to Berkeley as an adult. Her grandmother escaped the 1906 San Francisco earthquake and fire, rushing to the sanctity of

Oakland across the Bay, and saving en route to the ferryboat only—
goes the family lore—her fin de siècle fancy hats.

When I took a talk radio job in Los Angeles and moved us to
Santa Monica, Sheila made it clear that she felt she was moving into
foreign territory.

"I think it all started with a trip to L.A. in my youth," she explained
later when I asked her why she favored splitting the state. "Seeing
women in shorts, fur coats, and high heels made me realize their values
were different than mine. Hollywood and that whole cinematic scene,"
she insisted, "is not what California should mean." Her aversion to the
south was not just theoretical. "Later on, when movie stars started being
elected to high office, that proved it." Or as Randy Newman sings in "I
Love L.A.," what the Los Angeles Times calls The Southland is another
world, a world where he can "crank up the Beach Boys" as he's "rolling
down the Imperial Highway, a big nasty redhead at my side."

But Sheila is not alone, and as late as 2011 still another of the
myriad brainstorms to chop up California was proposed, this one
from Riverside County supervisor Jeff Stone. Supervisor Stone campaigned for Riverside and a dozen surrounding counties to secede
and form South California. His map lacks what offended Sheila and
constitutes southern California for much of the world: Los Angeles. That's because Stone sees L.A. as a variation on Sheila's Berkeley, embracing "the same liberal policies that Sacramento does." He
wanted the coast side liberals to be North California and the inland
to be his South. Maybe more appropriate nomenclature for his split
would be Left California and Right California. Stone called California "ungovernable" and lamented what he considered a soft-on-
illegal-immigration policy as an example.[1] In its story about Stone's
South California idea, the New York Times counted over two hundred calls for splitting up California since statehood in 1850, and
noted the glib reaction of Stone's fellow Riverside County supervisor, board chairman Bob Buster. "We're already balkanized in this

state," said Buster. "The problem is governance itself, but we need to work to fix the problems, not spend time talking about just taking our marbles and leaving."[2]

Secession. It sounds like such an obvious solution to so many problems. Although another Confederacy-type secession from the Union would likely result in a Civil War–like response from Washington, territory within a state can secede legally from its state and form another. Just ask Vermont, Delaware, and West Virginia, for three examples. All it takes post–Civil War is statewide agreement and a nod from Washington—but those simple requirements are much easier to yell from a soapbox than to accomplish once the time comes to count votes. Back in the 1950s, San Luis Valley residents considered quitting Colorado and becoming New Mexicans.[3] Not long after independence from King George, Connecticut and Pennsylvania settlers shot at each other for the contested Wyoming Valley.[4] As recently as 2011, efforts continued to create a South Florida and a North Florida. "We'd have same-sex marriage. They'd have a defense-of marriage act," was the enthusiastic campaign slogan coined by *Sun Sentinel* columnist Michael Mayo from his Ft. Lauderdale headquarters. "We'd have the Keys," he enthused. "They'd have the Redneck Riviera."[5] Cook County was promoted as a separate state by lawmakers claiming frustration with Chicago-style politics "dictating its views" to the rest of Illinois.[6] There was a West Kansas Movement in 1992.[7] The Eastern Shore periodically wants to split from Maryland.[8] And, of course, all those southern states did secede—ultimately unsuccessfully—during the Civil War, after failing to woo California into the Union as a slave state.

The *Times* article from 2011 on South California cited the well-publicized 1941 State of Jefferson attempt at independence as the closest to fruition any of those two-hundred-plus efforts at cutting up California came to creating a breakaway state. It's an understandable conclusion, perhaps, after looking at the newspaper photograph of one of the roadblocks (is it the one placed by local protesters or the one planted by newsreel photographers?). The protesters stopped traffic just south of Yreka on Highway 99 and gave passersby a copy of Jefferson's "Proclamation of Independence." Maybe old newsreel footage of Jefferson's newly "elected" Governor John C. Childs celebrating after his inauguration speech in Yreka convinced the *Times* that the Jefferson statehood movement was credible.

The incredible Jefferson reality, as we learn, is ongoing and more complicated, comical, deadly serious, and more germane for our era than most observers imagine. Come with me now as we meet the Jeffersonians, and see if you don't agree that their struggle for independence—real or mythical—is one we all share, at least now and then.

Select Dramatis Personae (in order of appearance)

The elusive State of Jefferson itself must be listed as the lead character in this story: Jefferson, that amorphous entity between California and Oregon that's fueled so many Wild West dreams of independence (from what?).

Mayor **Gilbert Gable,** struck down in his prime from overwork (or over drink?) just as the tireless Port Orford, Oregon, booster was about to add pseudo-governor to his title.

Ace reporter **Stanton Delaplane,** Pulitzer Prize winner and Irish coffee popularizer, a swashbuckler equally at ease with fact and fiction.

San Francisco Chronicle editor **Bill German,** quick to appreciate his reporter's turns of phrase and creativity, unconcerned about the provenance of legendary quotes.

Crescent City judge **John C. Childs,** the one and only governor of the State of Jefferson, self-appointed and self-anointed.

Model A Ford aficionado **Brian Favero,** whose father was one of the secessionists manning the Highway 99 barricades.

Contemporary Port Orford mayor **James Auborn,** wistful still that his predecessor never managed to build a railroad link to their coastal paradise.

Del Norte County sheriff **Dean Wilson,** happy to see you swaggering down the streets of Crescent City, your six-gun on your belt in flagrant violation of California law.

Former California assemblyman **Stan Statham,** dedicating his golden years to splitting the Golden State into at least two.

Jefferson merchant **Rick Jones,** his general store stocked with Jefferson flags, Jefferson bumper stickers, and Jefferson license plate frames.

Jefferson trailer park proprietor **Bruce Johnson,** looking at his empty trailer spaces while blaming his neighbors, the Karuk tribe.

Karuk biologist **Ken Brink,** struggling to save the Klamath River coho salmon fishery.

Klamath County commissioner **Tom Mallams,** elected on a platform that calls for the dismantling of the Endangered Species Act.

Journalist **Liz Bowen,** rousing the rabble via her website Pie N Politics.

Retiree **Anthony Intiso,** working hard to prevent his adopted homeland from becoming a National Monument.

Winnemem Wintu chief **Caleen Sisk,** striving to bring salmon back to the McCloud River and modesty back to the tribe's coming-of-age ceremony.

Radio newsman **Geoffrey Riley,** broadcasting on Jefferson Public Radio, defying state borders via the airwaves.

YouTube Jeffersonian **Charles Walker,** yelling at his followers to secede, from his bunker somewhere in Jefferson.

Former miner **Richard Stumbo,** fueling gold fever from his supply house just off the Rogue River.

Oregon founding father General **Joseph Lane,** riding off to the Jefferson Indian wars before running for vice president of the United States on a pro-slavery ticket.

Environmentalist **George Sexton,** worried from his Ashland refuge that Jefferson's divisiveness is dangerous, even as he struggles to salvage what wild land is left.

Museum curator **Michael Crane,** seeking Jefferson's identity through art.

T-shirt salesman **Ryan Casad,** happy to sell you a Jefferson double cross–emblazoned T-shirt, yet remarkably unclear on the concept.

The wandering minstrels who call their band the **State of Jefferson,** and sing odes to the 51st state.

Greta Garbo who, like so many Jeffersonians, is famous for saying, "I want to be alone."

And yours truly, dear reader, your humble guide through the bizarre world of the State of Jefferson.

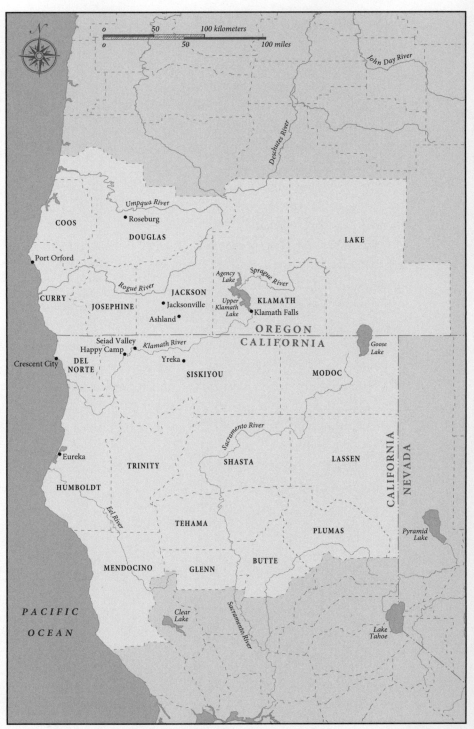

Visions of Jefferson's borders differ throughout the elusive state's history. This depiction of a Greater Jefferson extends the rouge state far east into the Oregon high desert and tauntingly south along the Sacramento River toward California's capital city.

Chapter One

En Route to Port Orford: Jefferson's Lost Capital

THE OBVIOUS PLACE TO START PROBING THE ORIGINS AND STATUS of Jefferson is in Yreka, the once and perhaps present capital city of the presumptive state.

It is in the *Yreka Mountain Herald* where I've found the earliest recorded announcement of a secessionists' conspiracy. In the January 14, 1854 edition of the newspaper—less than four years after California became the 31st state and just over five years before Oregon became the 33rd—a notice headlined "Siskiyou Mass Meeting" called on citizens to meet in the Yreka Hotel that Saturday evening "for the purpose of taking measures to secure the formation at an early day of a new territory out of certain portions of Northern California and Southern Oregon." A supportive adjacent letter to the editor argues in favor of the idea with a simple plea: "Let us then have a New Territory, and let power, civil and military, pass into hands who understand our wants and will, and let them wield it in subservitence [*sic*] to our wishes."

Even before California became a state there were suggestions it should be cut into smaller political entities. In 1978 Assembly Bill 2929, introduced by Assemblyman Barry Keene (and cosponsored by fourteen of his colleagues, including Stan Statham who relentlessly promotes splitting the state), called for the "consent of the Legislature" to the secession of much of the north part of the state. "The new state shall be known as 'Alta California' and shall consist of that territory lying north of a line representing the crest of the Tehachapi Mountain Range and extended therefrom west to the Pacific Ocean and east to the eastern boundary of the State of California," read the bill's legalese. "The State of California," promised the legislators, "shall retain the name 'California' and shall consist of all territory south of the new state."

The bill died, but a footnote to it adds some perspective to the history of dividing California. It reminds us that the first attempt was when California was still Mexican territory, back in 1825 (just four years after liberation from Spanish rule), and that despite the fact that most contemporary split talk is instigated in the north, southerners called for separation in 1852 on through 1859, and again in 1907. Another footnote to Barry Keene's state-splitting legacy is indicative of the distaste many of us from northern California feel for our southern Californian brethren. When Keen was asked about the locales for capital cities of the two Californias, he agreed that the north should keep Sacramento since it likely would fall in northern territory. As for the south, "That's their problem," he said. "I suggest Disneyland."[9]

Today travelers racing up Interstate 5 toward Yreka from Sacramento and points south cannot miss the huge letters screaming STATE OF JEFFERSON painted on the roof of a hay barn that faces oncoming freeway traffic. The dramatic announcement is credited to longtime Jefferson booster, the late Brian Helsaple, who lived in nearby Seiad Valley—where the general store flies the Jefferson state flag. Despite the WalMart and strip malls on the edge of the city, Yreka's old downtown abides. At the corner of Broadway and Miner Street, the Chamber of Commerce occupies a storefront and offers passersby State of Jefferson paraphernalia: baseball caps, tote bags, T-shirts, and flags—all sporting the trademark double X emblazoned on a miner's pan that is Jefferson's "official" state seal, dating from 1941. Those two X's were designed to represent Sacramento and Salem double-crossing Jefferson, and were painted on the mining pan to remind California and Oregon of Jefferson's mineral riches.

But rather than starting my quest in Yreka, I decided to come looking for Jefferson from the north, heading down the Oregon coast to Jefferson's almost capital, Port Orford. Along with that almost-the-capital status, lonely Port Orford is the westernmost municipality in the continental United States of America. Perhaps it was the relative proximity to Japan that attracted the World War II attack on nearby Curry County forestlands—the only place on mainland America Japanese forces managed to fly over and bomb (a bizarre only-in-Jefferson story too good not to tell).

Sheila at my side (blonde, not a Randy Newman redhead), we escaped the triple digit temperatures of the Willamette Valley summer, seeking not just relief from the heat but a change of the wallpaper. Changing wallpaper as a metaphor for moving is a saying I first encountered living in Berlin, a city (and nation) divided by victors— a forced secession that resulted in radically different German cultures developing post–World War II. The differences lingered well past the early 1990s reunification. Germans called their split personalities the *Mauer im Kopf*, the wall in the head. Always glib Oscar Wilde is credited with recognizing the value of wallpaper as he was lying on his deathbed in a Paris hotel, surrounded by décor not to his liking. His last words, according to legend: "Either that wallpaper goes or I do."

The day started wrong. Searching for a lost contact lens, I opened the P-trap under the upstairs bathroom sink to paw through the brown slimy gunk packed on its insides, no contact in sight. Then the sink drain plug opened before I replaced the trap, showering me with the mucky water. We finally headed south on I-5 to Cottage

Grove and a lunch-to-go at Busters, named for Buster Keaton (scenes for *The General*—his Civil War romantic adventure film—were shot in Cottage Grove and its environs).

"Oregon is so America," Californian Sheila says, looking at the iceberg lettuce in her sandwich as evidence.

We leave the freeway at Drain (appropriate, given the morning bathroom sink adventure) and head west on State Route 38 to the guaranteed cooler temperatures at the coast. Seventy-four degrees at Reedsport. Down US 101 to Curry County and as we approach Port Orford the bright sun becomes mottled by incoming fog as the temperature drops into the fifties. Relief. We're in Jefferson. But there are no outward signs of such a place.

Unlike Yreka, Port Orford offers no obvious suggestion that we've arrived in Jefferson. Yet if there is any one character in this story who can stake a claim to being the George Washington of Jefferson, it must be Port Orford's first mayor, Gilbert C. Gable—even though he died just days before local boosters declared Jefferson free of California and Oregon. I've arrived at this fogbound, desolate-looking outpost in search of the character, or at least his legacy.

Coastal Highway 101 widens to four lanes at the city limits, four empty lanes: There's no traffic here. We pass Dana's Trading Post and its hopeful sign offering us NEW USED BUY SELL TRADE—a sign facing an empty parking lot. What does Dana "new used buy sell trade"? CARDS, GIFTS, SOUVENIRS, SHIRTS, SWEETS, INCENSE AND YANKEE CANDLES, another sign implores. In front of The Crazy Norwegian's Fish & Chips, somebody's nightmare RV sits, rusting in the weeds. The Grantland Mayfield Gallery needs a fresh coat of paint, but its wood-frame facade dates from Port Orford's earliest days and looks to me as if it would fit comfortably in New England. The fading blue with white trim probably adds to its East Coast reflection, but the sign in a second floor window is pure Jeffersonian: THE RICH STEAL, it warns. POLITICIANS LIE. A sign on the marquee at Driftwood

Elementary School confirms hard times. KIDS FREE LUNCH JUNE 11 TO AUG 2 MON-THUR 11:30-12:15. A block from the Democratic Party headquarters, flags festoon an ad hoc red, white, and blue sign with another political warning: TO PROTECT OUR LIBERTY & THE U.S. CONSTITUTION DEFEAT OBAMA 2012. A forlorn sign calls out PHARMACY from an empty storefront, its metal awning dripping with rust, a lonely beach ball in its show window. There is a phone booth in front of Port Orford's sole grocery store; not everyone owns a cell phone. Don Rey's Mexican Food (NOW SERVING COCA-COLA) offers a "drive thru" window. And six dusty lava lamps adorn the window at the *Port Orford News*—I take it as an indicator that things don't change too rapidly in these parts these days.

City Hall shares squat quarters with the police department. But there is legacy and history at the building. A sign out front identifies that the MAYOR GILBERT E. GABLES COUNCIL CHAMBERS is inside, and a plaque notes that the construction of those chambers was funded by one Robert E. Gable—that would be the mayor's son. I had talked to Bob that morning on the phone from his summer place on Lake Michigan. He sounded at least mildly amused that I reached him from a research trip to Port Orford. We're scheduled to meet in Kentucky come wintertime for more stories promised about his father's Pacific coast dreams and to catalogue Jefferson memorabilia still at the family's Frankfort homestead.

Now I want to get into the city hall to check out the portrait of Mayor Gable in the chambers, but it's the weekend and the doors are locked. Rural America remains accessible. I find the current mayor's cell phone number on the city's website and give him a ring. Mayor James Auborn picks up the phone and I ask him if he might consider coming downtown to the city hall so I can take a look inside. He'd be happy to, he says, except he's up in Portland and won't be back until after a dentist appointment in Eugene on Monday. There is no dentist's practice in his hometown. We agree to meet at his dentist's office in a few days for a chat. Meanwhile he gives me the city administrator's phone number, who calls the lone police officer on duty, and after the cop finishes writing out a ticket he returns to headquarters to help. Officer Levi Esalon greets me with a smile, stocky-looking in his bulletproof vest, a pistol and a Taser on his belt—but he soon realizes he is equipped with no key to the council chambers.

I was looking at back issues of *Port Orford Today* to make sure I spelled Officer Esalon's name correctly and ran across the "Police Chief's Report" column and the news that the Bend, Oregon, police department donated three used cruisers to Port Orford. "Our only costs will be placing new graphics on these cars and changing some of the radio equipment before they can hit the streets," wrote Chief Marvin Combs in his column, proud to report the news about the "newer" squad cars for his department. "I want to thank the City of Bend and Police Chief Sandy Baxter for donating the equipment to our agency." What was wrong with these old cars that made them unfit for duty in Bend? How does Port Orford feel about depending on hand-me-down cop cars to chase bad guys? It reminds me of seeing antiquated Gringo school buses doing past-their-prime duty hauling paying passengers down in Mexico, and aged London double-deckers, patches of sheet metal clanking and their trademark red long faded, plying the streets of Peshawar, Pakistan, packed with people. Maybe Bend is so wealthy it's like a kindly uncle giving his struggling nephew last year's Cadillac instead of trading it in when he buys his new one. Which suggests Bend really must be fat and happy if it didn't need to sell those three old cars, and that Port Orford really is struggling if it is anxious to make do with the cast-off squad cars.

City administrator Mike Murphy is busy splitting firewood he's donating to benefit the local food co-op. I call him again; the key to the chambers is on his key ring. He's got no time to come downtown with the keys; there's a pile of wood to split. But he offers a solution. If I drive about a dozen miles north to where he's operating the splitter, he'll give me his keys to the council chambers so I can wander around and capture some photographs. When I'm finished, he instructs me to slip the keys into the public utilities payment box on the sidewalk in front of City Hall. Ah, small town America trusts. Imagine the mayor of Salem or Sacramento offering the city hall keys to a strange journalist wandering around their capital cities.

Chapter Two

An Introduction to
Hick Mayor Gilbert Gable

Once inside I admire Mayor Gable's official portrait, a photograph hanging on the wall behind the city councilors' chairs, and centered between the American and Oregon flags. He looks almost movie-star-handsome, staring with what seems like melancholy acceptance at the camera, the wide suitcoat lapels and slicked-back hair both anchoring him in the late 1930s or early 1940s. Rules posted for use of what's known as the Gable Chambers reinforce the small town atmosphere. If you have coffee, drinks and/or food, reads rule number one, please lift the plastic bag out of the trash can and take your trash with you. It could sit there for two or three days, and it smells. In a display case is a reminder of one of Gilbert Gable's earlier careers: an announcement from his agent, the Famous Speakers Bureau, saying that he is just back from the American Southwest and available to lecture for a fee. "Probably no living man has gone happily and delightfully through an experience more packed with spectacular achievement in explorations, scientific discoveries and the romance of pioneering adventure," exudes the brochure. It promises that Gable will tell stories of finding the world's largest trove of dinosaur tracks and a lost Indian city while finding time to experience "native religious rites as a brother of the tribe." The City Hall tribute belies Mayor Gable's modest characterization of himself just a couple of days

Gilbert Gable's image presiding over the Port Orford Council Chambers.

before he died as "the hick mayor of the Westernmost city of the United States."[10]

I lock up the Council Chambers and the city hall, drop the key into the bill box as instructed, and head for my lodgings. "Look for the words 'Ocean View' on the road," the proprietor of the Castaway by the Sea Motel told me when I reserved a room. I chose the Castaway both for the ocean view and because it shares grounds overlooking the port with the remnants of the Castaway by the Sea Lodge. Built in 1935, the lodge served first as the headquarters for the Trans-Pacific and Port Orford Dock and Terminal Company, one of Gilbert Gable's dashed business dreams. The rough seas destroyed his deep-water jetty, a barrier that created a harbor he expected would generate lucrative and efficient shipping traffic. There is no bar at Port Orford, so pilots are not needed to navigate a dangerous harbor entrance as is the case at ports up and down the Pacific coast. But the harbor faces the often-treacherous sea unprotected. Today the small local fishing fleet uses hoists to lift boats out of the Pacific and up onto the pier where, between voyages, they stay high and dry, safe from the crashing surf.

As I head south past the Paradise Café and the new library (built and paid for, I learn later, with funds generated by local volunteers), I see the arrow and huge white letters painted on a distant rise along the road. It does indeed say OCEAN VIEW. It neglects to add, "Unless it's so foggy you cannot see the hood ornament on your car." Which it was. Heavy windshield wiper wet fog. Rockne Berger graciously upgraded us to a sprawling apartment with a wall of windows overlooking what he guaranteed was the harbor. Coos Bay native Berger took me on a tour of Gable's old offices, most of which burned to the ground in what Berger labeled an arson fire set by a previous owner as an attempt to gain insurance money. Trouble was, goes the story, the perpetrator took all the elegant and valuable furniture out of the lodge prior to torching it. Insurance denied. All that's left of the original complex are two soaring fireplace chimneys reclaimed by fauna and flora, and one wing of the old lodge that Berger rents to vacationers.

On display in the vestigial lodge are examples of Gilbert Gable's promotional prose—in addition to explorer, his previous careers included public relations. He plied that trade for several years in Philadelphia at Bell Telephone. "Vessels may enter or leave under any weather condition," he enthused about Port Orford on the displayed publicity brochure, advertising copy written prior to the mayor losing his wharf during typically severe and treacherous Pacific weather. "Practically free from the prevailing fogs of the Pacific Coast," he claimed about Port Orford, as I thought about my hood ornament disappearing in the thick wet fog. A framed menu from 1950 offers a full barbecue crab dinner with soup and salad, coffee, and dessert for $2.25. Roast turkey costs the same. Add a dollar for a T-bone, New York, tenderloin, or top sirloin steak, which comes with a crab cocktail and potatoes, too. Testimonials fill the menu along the lines of, "Never had a better time in my life," E. K., Basel, Switzerland. As anonymous as Yelp.

Dinner for us was a few blocks distant at Redfish, perched—though the now dripping fog obscured it—on a cliff over the ocean. The elegant eatery is an anomaly on the Port Orford strip. It would fit comfortably in Portland's Pearl District or my hometown, Sausalito. The waiters could practice some decorum. "Hard to decide," one announced to us as we studied the menu. "Everything is so wonderful." Redfish is as far from the down market Paradise Café as it is from the 1950 menu hanging on the wall up at the lodge. Steak these days at the upscale eatery goes for $34, and the burger is more than twice what they charge at the Paradise (but then the Paradise doesn't caramelize Walla Walla onions for you, and instead of the Redfish's goat cheese your cheese choice at the Paradise is American or Swiss). Sheila and I split the grilled chinook and we washed it down with a nice Willamette Valley white from the Sokol Blosser winery.

Chapter Three

A Rugged Coast's Rugged History

That night I couldn't get to sleep. I sat in the Castaway living room thinking about Gilbert Gable. Was he crazed to think this isolated spot halfway between Portland and San Francisco could be another major West Coast port? A visionary? A hustler? Or all three? It's easy to second-guess his ambition from my vantage point in this desolate-looking stretch of fogbound coastline. But at the time when Gable saw a grand future for Port Orford, the place was bustling with a vibrant fishery and a timber industry busy exporting Port Orford cedar.

No longer.

"Unless your family is in cranberries or owns a fishing boat," Rockne Berger told me when we were touring the old lodge grounds, "the best thing for high school graduates is to get out of here."

The locale, according to tourist information I find in the apartment, saw its first white settlers in 1851 (just three years before that first suggestion over in Yreka that Jefferson be carved out of Oregon and California). They came from Portland via the sea, looking for gold and timber. Local Native Americans engaged the immigrants in combat at what is now known as Battle Rock. The whites sought escape overland back toward the north. Battle Rock was littered with dead and wounded.

Throughout the 1850s the Indians and white settlers fought over Jefferson land and its use. The settlers wanted to farm and mine the natives' ancestral home territories. When I returned to Eugene I sat in the somber special collections reading room in the University's Knight Library, reading through the Cayuse, Yakima, and Rogue River Wars papers. The collection of original letters written by soldiers, politicians, businessmen, and farmers brings the genocide perpetrated in my neighborhood into stark relief. As the library's own summary of its primary sources concludes: "Many tribal members succumbed to either military attack or disease, and most of the remaining populations were sent to live on reservations." The carefully preserved letters are a reminder that the settlers suffered, too. This was brutal war. There are letters to and from newspaperman and Oregon Territory governor George L. Curry recounting details of ongoing conflict (an Indian massacre, an attack by settlers, stolen guns and animals). The correspondence makes the Wild West feel real and recent in the silence of the high-ceiled reading room.

I held a letter dated July 15, 1856, from Thomas Van Pelt to John K. Lamerick, a commander of the Oregon Volunteers. The elegant cursive is written in sepia ink (or faded to sepia by time?). "We have to take up our rifles and go fighting again," he writes, because "the redskins are not satisfied or whipped." He recounts fighting in the Coast Range between Crescent City and Port Orford. "They were fired upon by a party of Indians and two of them were kild [*sic*] on the spot." Van Pelt reports his fast response. "I immediately raised 20 men," and they headed "to the place of the slaughter, and found and buried the bodies of the 2 men." Van Pelt offered his military expertise to the war effort in exchange for a commission with the Volunteers. "I have had considerable experience in fighting Indians. My manner of fighting has always bin [*sic*] successful." He calls on Lamerick to "attend to this business immediately and relieve your fellow citizens on the coast of southern Oregon. If you comply with this important request, I will raise the men. With very much respect I remain your humble servant."[11]

Sitting on the couch in my Castaway living room in Port Orford, I look up from my musing and reading; I see lights on the fishing pier. The fog retreated in the dark, when I wasn't looking. At daybreak the sweeping coastline comes sparkling into sight. Rock outcroppings punctuate the ocean. On the cliffside, daisies and sweet peas brighten up the scene. Placid waters are washing up on the driftwood-covered beach below the apartment. There is blue in the sky. Lingering fog floats on the evergreen-covered headlands to the south. As did the Japanese aviator who bombed the forests here in 1942, I now can see this harsh and often unforgiving stretch of spectacular coastline. The attack seaplane came disassembled in a submarine. Stormy Oregon coast weather (surprise!) kept the boat and plane submerged for days until, as is the case this morning, the clouds broke and the rain stopped. The crew assembled the aircraft and Chief Flying Officer Nobuo Fujita took off on his bombing run with the apparent goal of igniting forest fires. No luck: The trees were wet with rainwater and the fires fizzled. Twenty years later Fujita came back for a visit bringing his family's samurai sword, which he gave to nearby Brookings as a peace gesture (but with which his daughter said he had intended to commit seppuku had Oregonians rejected his peace overture). Brookings citizens responded by making Fujita an honorary citizen.[12]

Chapter Four

Port Orford Pioneer Survivors

Time for breakfast. We drive off to the Paradise (and finally a hint of Jefferson—we listen to Jefferson Public Radio, broadcasting from over the mountains in Ashland, for the news). Sheila orders the one-half special: one egg, one slice of toast, and hashbrowns. A bargain at $3.75. You get what you pay for. Greasy hashbrowns and here—where we're surrounded by berry farms—a squat packet of Smucker's jam for the toast.

I've secured appointments with two longtime Port Orford residents for the morning. Dolores Mayea, who informs me when I ask for a Sunday morning appointment to come anytime because "I don't go to church," and ninety-three-year-old Lucille Douglass, who comes up with an even better line when I ask if we can meet. "I'm not going anywhere," she informs me.

Dolores Mayea lives along Garrison Lake, just a few blocks from the Highway 101 main drag through Port Orford—Oregon Street— and just east of the sand dunes that dominate so much of the Oregon coast. The lake was named for John B. Garrison, listed in some accounts as one of the original pioneers who came to what was not yet known as Port Orford in 1851 aboard the steamer *Sea Gull* (and who escaped north after the attacks at Battle Rock).[13] Hers is a 1950s-style ranch house that would look comfortable in the American suburbs anywhere. The mantel is lined with family photographs going back generations to a formal black and white study of her parents. Her father was born along the southern Oregon coast—a logger, rancher, and land developer. Her mother moved west with her family from Idaho, looking for work. This has been Mayea's home for sixty-one years, the place where she and her late husband raised five children—and all of them left Port Orford for lives lived elsewhere.

A handsome, robust woman in her mid-eighties, Dolores Mayea leans back in what looks like it must be her favorite chair, the sparkling lake providing a backdrop over her shoulders, and tells stories of a city that's disappearing—no jobs and no next generation. The kids get out of high school and they skedaddle. "There isn't any work here," she laments. "There are no more mills. There's no more anything. There's some fishing. But the regulations are just getting worse and worse and worse all the time." Her voice drops as she says with finality, "It's sad."

That seems an appropriate word for Port Orford: sad. One out-of-business storefront after another on Oregon Street, few jobs, and a brain and brawn drain all add up to sad no matter how spectacular the countryside looks.

The remnants of the Port Orford pharmacy.

"In the fifties we had all kinds of businesses." Mayea shows Sheila and me a couple of old newspapers from those days, the pages jammed with display advertising for local businesses. "When our kids were growing up we had a couple of dress shops, a shoe store, two grocery stores, three gas stations, a men's clothing store, restaurants. We had a wonderful drugstore, and a variety store."

"You could get what you needed without leaving town," I offer.

"Right. It has changed," she says with complete resignation, "considerably." She expresses no expectation that those glory days will return. "Art galleries, that's all we have anymore."

"What's it like," I ask, "to see the place where you've lived all your life deteriorate?" Deteriorate is the correct word. There is nothing much compelling about the streetscape in Port Orford, unless your eye is lured by the desolate and the dilapidated. Glimmers of renewal and prosperity on Oregon Street, like Redfish and the new library, such stark contrasts to the degraded commercial district, act as reminders that so much of the rest of Port Orford looks like a ghost town in the making.

"It's sad," she says again, a statement that seems odd given how delightful her home and its location appear. The devastated economy does not diminish the spectacular natural beauty of the place: soaring headlands, broad beaches, glorious sunsets (when the fog lifts!). To the south of the Mayea place, the road to the old Coast Guard station is lined with gracious homes, bargains by Portland and San Francisco standards. I found a sweet little three-bedroom bungalow built in 1940 on 9th Street listed at $139,000 and a more modern and sprawling three-bedroom by the lake for $188,500.

"I own a lot of property," my host points out, "and nothing is selling."

I mention the sign at the school offering free lunches and the talk turns political.

"I shouldn't say it," Dolores Mayea tells me and before I can encourage her to keep talking she adds, "but I will. I think there are a lot of people that really work the system. My husband," her voice rises, "if times were tough, he went out and cut fern or boughs or cut wood to sell. He never ever would ask for unemployment or any kind of assistance because, he said, his family was his responsibility, not anybody else's. That was how most of our generation—the people that we knew—that's how we all felt. Today," she says, sounding much like too many callers to my radio talk shows over the years, "I think there is too much government in our lives."

I take the bait and remind her that the Jefferson statehood movement was motivated by too little government. Mayor Gable and his contemporaries—and Mayea remembers the mayor from her childhood—wanted the government to build better roads in order to make exploitation of Jefferson's minerals and timber more efficient.

"And we still don't have adequate roads," she tells me.

"So we need the government!" I find myself in talk show host mode there in her living room, arguing the point.

She's quick with a Jeffersonian response. "But they spend the money where all the people are. So what good does government do us?"

"But you need Salem and Sacramento because the local economy is not self-sufficient," is my retort.

"I guess," is her resigned response, along with a laugh that signals she wants to change the subject. I'm her guest and I shut down my talk show personality.

"All my life I have heard Port Orford is going to grow, and it isn't as big as it used to be," she says.

I ask Dolores Mayea if she has a message for Mayor Gable's son, since I expect to meet with him soon back in Kentucky.

"I just wish his father had been more successful in his endeavors here," she says, "because I think there would have been a lot more here now than there is."

Sheila and I take our leave, but not before we're presented with a jar of home-canned tuna for the road. "I've canned a lot of things, but never tuna," Sheila said when Dolores Mayea was regaling us with tales of her family canning tuna. Small town America: friendly and hospitable.

Across the highway from Dolores Mayea's place and just down the street from the blue and white Grantland Mayfield Gallery is the faded glory of Lucille Douglass's house. It's a classic nineteenth-century Victorian-influenced two-story wood-frame structure sorely in need of paint and repair, a lot of paint and repair. Lace curtains decorate some windows; one is boarded up with a piece of plywood. Weeds fill the yard; the porch is out of plumb. Down in California the ghost town Bodie is kept in what the park rangers there call "an arrested state of decay." The Douglass relic's decay is not arrested—the gracious old house looks as if it is mighty close to the point where if it is not restored soon, it will be lost.

Lucille Douglass invited us in, blaming her bent body on a fall down the stairs, and warning us from expecting to learn much from her because she suffers from Alzheimer's disease. "The last two months," she insists, her voice strong and clear, her hair white, "I've lost my memory. With my sister in Seattle, that's all I talk about now. She thinks she's going the same way. Alzheimer's. A dirty word." She titters, that's the best word for the cynical laugh that follows her self-diagnosis. "Let's get back to Mayor Gable," she orders about our interview, showing no overt signs of dementia and acting like a woman accustomed to being in charge.

The newspaper edition Lucille Douglass saved.

"He was a doer," she says about Gable, although she only remembers meeting him, not knowing him. "I think I was still in high school when they dedicated the new jetty down there." That was 1935. "My memory is slipping. I'm going to use that as an excuse." We're sitting around a large dining table in a cluttered room. Two treadle sewing machines rest against one wall, one carrying the "Your New Home" brand name. She points to a drawer and offers me the opportunity to root around in it. "That's mom's filing cabinet. Grandpa Limbergh built it. He built this house. He built a bunch of them here." It's gorgeous, I say, thinking about what it was and could be. "It's gone downhill," is her appropriate response.

The drawer is full of family papers: birth and death certificates, that sort of thing. And tucked away in the family history is a yellowing copy of the *Port Orford Post*, dated December 5, 1941—in fine shape except for a few crumbles and tears. "Mayor Gilbert Gable Dies Suddenly Here" is the banner headline.

"Well, I'll be darned," she says, opening the paper and offering a "Whoops!" as a page of the yellowing artifact rips in her hands. "He succumbed to indigestion," she reports after glancing at the obituary.

Perhaps. Later, I hear from the current mayor that alcohol and a hard-drinking city slicker passing through town may have played a role.

But the December 5th *Post* ("From the most westerly city in the United States") does not speculate. "Death was attributed," the paper reports, "to an attack of acute indigestion brought on by a complete nervous fatigue the result of his indefatigable efforts to bring development to Curry county within the next few months." The mayor is survived, announces the obituary, by his widow, Paulina Stearns Gable, and one son, Bobbie, "a student in the Port Orford grade school."

"Little Bobbie Gable," muses Lucille Douglass as we prepare to leave her. "I remember him as a little boy. Nice kid."

Chapter Five

PORT ORFORD MAYORAL DREAMS: FROM PORTLAND TO CARMEL

BACK AT MY OFFICE, I READ THROUGH THE *PORT ORFORD POST* reports on Gable's death. The paper recounts his years as a publicist for Bell Telephone and the wartime Liberty Loan drives, his explorations in the Arizona desert (his discoveries: "the largest number of dinosaur tracks in the world and a lost Indian village"). After he married into the Stearns family (Michigan lumber), he used his adventures as fodder for his NBC radio series *Highroad to Adventure*. He came to the West in 1933, "his imagination fired by tales of this last frontier." He died "a man worn out in the prime of life by his ceaseless fight to bring development to the land he loved."

The paper quotes from an interview the editor conducted with Mayor Gable not long before he died. "I see it all so clearly now," Gable dreamed aloud about Port Orford, "as though I had focused the telescope of my life on one target that grows and grows until it finally has become almost too large for the glass. I see our breakwater that means Port Orford's harbor will become one of the greatest in the nation. I see Port Orford as one of the great fishing centers of the world, I see our natural minerals being developed and our people coming into their rightful place. For the first time I can see clearly the speedy fulfillment of our dreams and hopes."

What was, to use the current vernacular, the man smoking? Or, in this case perhaps, drinking? Gable evangelized that with government development cash, Port Orford could rival Portland and San Francisco. He wanted a breakwater to protect his city's deep-water port from the rough Oregon Pacific. He wanted a railroad across the Coast Range to interchange with the rest of the country. He wanted roads to gain efficient access to Jefferson's minerals and timber.

"I want you to preach that in our little newspaper," the mayor lectured the editor. "I want you to keep everlastingly spurring the hope of our people toward realization that the things we have been fighting for are coming true. We cannot fail!" The exclamation point was the editor's, not mine.

The *Post*'s 1941 obituary for Mayor Gable is written with majestic prose reminiscent of an American newspaper style from the previous century: majestic and romantic. "Another pioneer of southwest Oregon has passed on down the long trail blazed by sacrifice and toil—a pioneer in the sense that he dreamed and built for the future, for the spirit that dominated the pioneer is not measured in time," the paper mourns. The mayor, "who dreamed and fought to the end for the place in the sun he believed the rightful heritage of his adopted land, is gone. Gone with him is the dynamic leadership that within the last few years has blazoned the name of Curry County throughout the nation. Gone is the true friend of Port Orford, the pioneer in achievement in this far western land who gave his life in service, finally to rest, worn out by the ceaseless battle for his southwest Oregon—a battle at times he waged almost single-handed." The soaring, elegiac, and poetic eulogy continues down the front page of the paper, ending with a forlorn civic cry about Port Orford's future without Mayor Gable. "A dream of empire is ended. But high out on the heads that overlook the bay of Port Orford the spirit of Gilbert E. Gable will ever be the impelling force to spur the progress of his beloved southwest Oregon."[14]

The newspaper from that December 5th, 1941, just two days before Pearl Harbor, offers a glimpse of Port Orford life. *I Wanted*

Wings, with Ray Milland, William Holden, and Veronica Lake ("America's newest glamour girl raids the hearts of four flying aces") is playing at the Port Orford Theatre. Margie's Coffee House is offering a lunch special for a quarter and dinner for thirty-five cents. And the front-page paean to Gable mourns the loss of his "idealism that has for its purpose the happiness and contentment of his fellowman."

Hundreds of miles south, the *San Francisco Chronicle* scooped the *Post* by a day with news of the mayor's demise. "I suppose I was the last newspaperman to interview him," wrote the paper's Stanton Delaplane, who was back at his *Chronicle* desk after writing the series of reports on the Jefferson secession movement that would win the Pulitzer Prize for him and his paper. "A friendly, warm talk," Delaplane called his visit, "in a redwood cabin while the Oregon skies poured dark rain into the pine-covered hills." Gable, he surmised, probably knew that Jefferson would never become an independent state, but figured the massive publicity generated by threats to secede could force Salem and Sacramento to be more responsive to Jefferson's cries for help.

"The other night in Oregon," Delaplane's dispatch continued, "I accused him of being a romantic. I said, 'I'm going to write that Gilbert Gable is watching the sun go down each evening over the Pacific with a golden dream in his eyes.' And he laughed and said, 'That's newspaper stuff, all right.' He died yesterday of acute indigestion," Delaplane stuck with the official cause of death, but added, "and perhaps he was too tense." Referring to the national publicity Gable generated with his talk of Curry County secession from Oregon, Delaplane called the mayor "a pioneer who used the tools at hand to fulfill his dreams of the West as men a century ago used long rifles and axes to build the Nation. He had an historical future, not as a forty-ninth State Governor, but as one of the last pioneers."[15]

Over seventy years later, James Auborn is Port Orford mayor. His vision for his forlorn city does not mirror his predecessor's, but as he fantasizes it to me, it sounds just as dreamy, just as far-fetched and just as—to be blunt—nuts. Mayor Auburn doesn't see Port Orford as a rival to Portland and San Francisco. He knows there's no potential at this most westerly place on the Lower Forty-Eight for a world-class city and a global port. Mayor Auburn fancies windswept, fogbound, still-isolated Port Orford as the next Carmel-by-the-Sea. Mayor Auburn, like Mayor Gable before him, is no rube. He is a physicist with a PhD from Oregon State University. He spent years in the Navy and working for Bell Laboratories back east (and remember, Mayor Gable worked for Bell) before returning to Oregon and moving to Port Orford, the spot he chose years before as an ideal locale for retirement.

"I really fell in love with the place."

But it's hard to imagine he researched much when he decided to equate Port Orford with Carmel. According to Weather Channel statistics, Port Orford is wetter each average year than Carmel by—dramatic pause—over fifty-one inches of rain.[16] And what about Carmel's fine dining, the gracious architecture, the elegant shops, the romantic ambiance, the beaches, the sun—the warmth?

"The town has changed quite a bit since then," Mayor Auburn says thinking back to days when Gilbert Gable was the city's mayor. "I think back in the early 1940s we had more bars and saloons in town than we had churches and now it's reversed. We probably have more churches than bars."

Of course I ask him why.

"It was a lumbering town back then," he reminds me, noting the mills in the city that ran long hours, filled with thirsty workers. "There are no mills in town now. Our principal industry probably is fishing."

Wait a minute. I know fishermen. "Fishermen drink just as much as loggers," I insist.

"Yeah," agrees the mayor, who proves to be a droll comedian, "but they're all on their boats."

Despite his Carmel dreams, Mayor Auborn does not disagree when I describe Port Orford as feeling like a place passed by. As did Mayor Gable before him, he blames roads. Flourishing Gold Beach to the south and Bandon-by-the-Sea to the north enjoy quick and easy access to the inland I-5 corridor, the road that ties the West together from Vancouver to Tijuana. And size matters, says the mayor. With a population of around a thousand, Port Orford is about half the size needed for a self-sustaining community. City planners, he explains, figure a place needs a couple of thousand residents to support basic services: the drugstore and soda fountain, a dry cleaners and laundry, more than one grocery store. Even when the lumber mills were humming and the fishery was thriving, Port Orford could not attract that critical mass of two thousand citizens. Nonetheless, at Ray's Food Place, the local supermarket, a glance at its shelves indicates a diverse clientele—retirees and artists are replacing those blue-collar workers. Ray's stocks two different brands of tahini, along with the all-American fried chicken that's waiting patiently for customers and staying warm under supermarket heat lamps.

Mayor Auborn and I muse about Gilbert Gable's fabled role in Port Orford history; the mayor seems particularly taken with Gable's dream of connecting the lonely outpost to Grants Pass, Medford, Ashland, and the rest of America via his never-built Gold Coast Railroad.

"Unfortunately that idea died with Gilbert Gable when he passed away of a heart attack."

"Heart attack? The obituaries I read in the *Post* and the *Chronicle* claim indigestion killed him. Acute indigestion."

The current mayor doesn't hide his smile. "There are some pretty colorful stories about his passing."

"Do tell!"

"He was drunk out of his mind is the local lore. Yeah, he was suffering from indigestion. But there probably was a little alcohol involved in that also." The mayor laughs and then amends his remark. "Probably quite a bit of alcohol involved."

"Was that his reputation? Was he a hard-drinking man?"

"I think he was a hard-living man. I don't think he was a drunk, but he probably enjoyed his beverage."

Less than forty-eight hours before his fatal indigestion, the mayor was enjoying beverages with the famed big city newspaper-man from San Francisco. Stanton Delaplane arrived in Port Orford, the final dateline for his Jefferson news-gathering trip, and met with Mayor Gable. "Gable had got a hold of a bottle of 150 proof Hudson Bay rum," according to one version of that local lore recounted in *The American West* years later, "and they sampled it while the dark rain poured down."[17] Note how that historian described the Oregon precipitation with the same words Delaplane used in the story he filed about his meeting with Gable "in a redwood cabin while the Oregon skies poured dark rain into the pine-covered hills."

"It was really tragic," Mayor Auborn says about the unexpected death as it relates to contemporary Port Orford. "If he would have built that railroad, we would have a highway there now, and a quite different history. We would have been really connected to the rest of the state."

Not that Auborn over-romanticizes Gable's civic pride. "While he was doing things for Port Orford he was also doing things for himself. No question he took care of himself well. He used his political office to look out for himself. You could never do that these days," the mayor says about his own role in City Hall.

"No back room deals today?"

"I'm not able to enrich myself by being the mayor. That's just the way things were. Things are different now."

One difference is the bleak main street with its empty store-fronts and dilapidated buildings. Mayor Auborn blames a block of no-growth voters who are happy to keep Port Orford a backwater where they can loll about in peace and quiet. But he offers a litany of examples, like the Redfish restaurant, of thriving businesses working to dress up downtown despite the naysayers.

"We have a bunch of people in town we call CAVE people, Citizens Against Virtually Everything." He laughs about the anti-growth faction and identifies a woman who moved to Port Orford about a dozen years ago and works hard to block the kind of growth and change that the mayor advocates. "She likes the isolation. She's got hers and she doesn't want anybody else coming in."

The conflicts between factions play out around issues such as the mayor's campaign to upgrade the city's water distribution system. The no-growth advocates decried the campaign, he says, claiming it was a veiled growth grab and that thousands of new water hook-ups would come to service the town.

"Nothing like that was going to happen," I offer, unable to imagine Port Orford attracting multitudes of immigrants. "That was a ridiculous claim." But I note in his complaints about obstructionist constituents a distinct parallel to national politics. "With only a thousand residents you suffer divisiveness just like the rest of America these days."

"Yeah, it's like Congress," he says about his city council. But he's convinced, just as was Gilbert Gable, that the future is bright for Port Orford. More Californians with progressive ideals and ideas are coming to town looking for bargain real estate. "If we can clean up some of the old buildings," he dreams. "If we could get a pharmacy back. We had a pharmacy when I first moved here. We could support one because our older population really needs the services of a pharmacy."

Dolores Mayea had told me it annoyed her to be forced to go to Bandon to fill her prescriptions.

"We could probably support a doctor and a dentist. There are people in town who have money."

But Port Orford's government struggles to provide services. Just as it was in the heyday of the 1941 Jefferson separatist movement, Salem is the current villain, and the mayor ticks off examples. The state won't allow the city to levy a surcharge on traffic tickets. An extra municipal gas tax is forbidden. The city is forced to comply with environment protection laws irrelevant to its rural setting.

I told Mayor Auborn I was traveling back east to meet with Mayor Gable's son. "Any message for him?"

"You can tell him that the current mayor still has progressive visions for Port Orford. And tell him we wish his dad had built that railroad. That would have made Port Orford quite different." He pauses for a few seconds before he thinks to add, "Maybe I wouldn't have liked it here as well if that railroad had been built," and he laughs.

"I remember walking back from school with a little girl." Robert Gable is reminiscing with me at the dining room table in his gracious Kentucky home. But he can't remember her name. Maybe it was Dolores. I traveled to Frankfort to meet with Gable and search through the archives he keeps that are filled with his father's papers. He was seven years old when his father Mayor Gilbert Gable died. But over seventy years later, he enjoys fond memories of a bucolic Port Orford childhood. "I remember white mice in a cage," he says about the family home, and the woods adjacent to it. "The woods that went over to the lumber yard and there were paths in the woods. We used to go out and play war with rubber band guns. This was just prior to World War II. Once December 7th hit and he had died, we moved to Tucson, where my grandmother was living. This gal's mother." He gestures to a framed formal portrait that fills a wall of the room. "I remember puddles in the unpaved road between the school and the house where I used to sail little boats. I remember some little girl skipping along with me. We were holding hands and she was singing, 'I'm walking with the mayor's son, the mayor's son, the mayor's son!'" He's little Bobbie Gable again, singing at his dining room table and smiling at the memory. "And that was the first time really I'd thought about it."

Robert Gable is a charming gentleman. We study the archive index and mark documents germane to Jefferson. After we talk Port Orford memories for about an hour, we adjourn to the garage and search through boxes until we find a draft typescript of a letter Mayor Gable wrote to Oregon governor Charles Sprague—a direct precursor to the push for statehood. "Has the state of Oregon," he asks, "done any geological or mineral development work in Curry County since President Roosevelt declared a state of emergency? If so, where? Does the governor honestly believe that the state department of Geology and Mining Industries is adequately staffed to meet the ever-increasing demands upon it in this national emergency? With gigantic defense contracts being let and plants being erected, has the case of Oregon—vast storehouse of vital defense materials— been placed before every federal agency in a sincere effort to win for our state the place she should command by virtue of her strategic defense materials?"

Governor Sprague responded with a letter back to the mayor dated November 15, 1941. "I do want you and the people of Curry County to feel that the state of Oregon does not want to neglect that section. We have built at great expense the Coast Highway through Curry County." The governor cites his interest in the development of mineral resources in southwestern Oregon, but doesn't consider his administration responsible for initiating such work. "I am sure," he writes about two weeks before the attack on Pearl Harbor, "if the emergency deepens and the need for strategic minerals increases, that the Government will reach out to utilize domestic supplies not now developed."

Mayor Gable was not mollified.

Chapter Six

Mayor Gable Pimps Statehood

The 1941 Jefferson escapade began in earnest October 2nd. A group of frustrated businessmen—inspired to act by Mayor Gable—addressed a session of the Curry County court at a meeting in Gold Beach, the county seat. The movers-and-shakers were seeking redress for their complaints about poor roads. Easy access to the county's natural resources—particular metals of value for the expected upcoming war effort—was impossible. The petitioners blamed the bad roads on disregard of Curry County by those Salem politicians representing the rest of Oregon. The court named a commission (Mayor Gable, of course, included) to study the complaints and Gable's attention-getting secession idea. The publicity-savvy mayor publically floated his brainstorm: join Curry County to California in hopes of getting better treatment from Sacramento than the passed-by county was getting from Salem. Culbert Olson, California's governor, was bemused when he heard the news, offering a sound bite that set the stage for the upcoming secession show when he said he was "glad to know they think enough of California to want to join it."[18]

In Portland, the *Oregonian* mocked the news in an editorial titled "Curry Beware." The newspaper warned of unintended consequences. "If ambition be realized, Curry would of course immediately acquire the glorious climate of California and become a haven for retired mid-west farmers; development of its mineral riches would add much more to the population. Gold Beach would become a metropolis with offensive slums, and Latin quarters, and traffic problems and police scandals and what not to cause dislike of it throughout the hinterland. Whereupon the hinterland would logically secede from Gold Beach." The editorial concluded with a snide plea. "The Curry county plan to become a county of California is so full of potential disaster that once again its people are beseeched to pause and consider."[19]

Dismissing the public derision, a meeting was called for Yreka. There Mayor Gable rallied representatives from Del Norte and Siskiyou Counties on the California side to join what became his movement for independence now that Governor Olson had snubbed his overture to become a Californian. The Yreka Chamber of Commerce voted to study statehood for the loose alliance. Next on the statehood bandwagon was the local organization of young civic leaders, the Yreka 20-30 Club. Its members announced that the confederation would secede on Thursdays in "patriotic rebellion" against Oregon and California.

Enter Stanton Delaplane, the San Francisco scribe who knew that there are no slow news days, only slow news reporters.

Chapter Seven

NEVER LET THE FACTS STAND IN THE PATH OF A GOOD STORY

STANTON DELAPLANE WAS A REPORTER IN THE TRADITION OF THAT classic tale of newspapering, the Ben Hecht and Charles MacArthur play, *The Front Page*. His was a world populated by figures like the fictional star reporter Hildy, who promised his fiancée in the Billy Wilder film version, "I'm going to cut out drinking and swearing and everything connected with the crazy newspaper business! Honey, I'll never even read a newspaper."

I grew up reading the *San Francisco Chronicle* during its rollicking period of making as much news with its publicity stunts as it reported from the front lines of breaking news. During the paper's heyday it was impossible to imagine starting a San Francisco day without reading the always-entertaining broadsheet—even as we loyal readers disparaged the paper for its superficial coverage of the world. The *Chronicle* was staffed by a stable of extraordinary creative writers, such as Delaplane. One of his stories, about a streetcar operator named Francis Van Wie, a man with multiple wives, was supported by a typical *Chronicle* whimsical headline: "The Ding-Dong Daddy Of The D Car Line." While conducting research for this book, my colleague Charles Deitz corresponded with longtime San Francisco reporter Lynn Ludlow, who interviewed Delaplane in 1980 for a nostalgic story about what the competing *Examiner* called the "Carbarn Casanova" and the *Call-Bulletin* referred to as the "Trolley Troubadour."

"When I mentioned that the celebrated polygamist never worked on the D car line but was a conductor instead on the F streetcars," Ludlow wrote to Deitz, "Stan acknowledged calmly that 'D' was more alliterative."

Delaplane also enjoyed the instant credibility of his creative writing. "I got a lot of mail from people who knew him, remembered him perfectly," he told Ludlow, "because they rode the D car line all the time. Heh, heh." Ludlow noted in his story, "Such was the power of the press, however, that even Van Wie started telling people he worked on the D car line."[20]

Bill German edited the newspaper's stories about Mayor Gable and his nascent statehood movement. I'm off to San Francisco this summer morning to see the ninety-something-year-old retired editor and to learn more about the stories behind Delaplane's dispatches. "I was one of Del's editors in the exciting year of 1941," he wrote as we were arranging to meet. I want editor German's take on the rumor I'd been picking up that it was Delaplane who wrote the State of Jefferson's famous "Proclamation of Independence" for the secessionists and that it was Delaplane who suggested that they throw a roadblock across Highway 99, both to help out the cause and to provide himself with good copy for the *Chronicle*.

Thirty-one thousand feet over Jefferson en route to the meeting with Delaplane's editor on a clear summer day, I look out on the 51st state. The remoteness of the region is obvious from the air. The pilot is following the I-5 corridor south and except for periodic sprawl at highway interchanges, from the I-5 freeway to the Pacific the coast range shows few signs of habitation or development in Jefferson's rugged mountains and isolated valleys. Here and there a road penetrates west and along it a cluster of buildings, surrounded by the rigid geometric patterns of cultivated land, indicates a settlement. Not that this looks like virgin territory. The forested mountainsides are pocked with huge swatches of bare spots. From the air these scars left by logging clear-cuts look like places on a scalp shaved for a brain operation—raw, with evidence of trauma. But as the miles whoosh by at five hundred something per hour, from the window at seat 7F on this United flight the impression is comforting: Most of Jefferson remains wild and free. Not to minimize the conflicts on the ground—farmers versus fishers, natives versus settlers, and environmental activists versus dredging gold miners and frustrated loggers. But from this aerial vantage point I find myself singing silently, "Give me land/lots of land/and the starry sky above/Don't fence me in," and thinking Robert Fletcher's 1934 lyrics, made popular by Cole Porter for the film *Don't Fence Me In*, would make an ideal Jefferson anthem.

Bill German went to work for the *San Francisco Chronicle* in 1940 as a copy boy, immediately after finishing his studies at the Columbia University Graduate School of Journalism. He spent his entire career—sixty-two years—at the paper, leading it as editor through its *Front Page* days in the mid-twentieth century when it called itself "The Voice of the West" and was required reading in San Francisco and throughout northern California for amusement as much as for the news of the day. The *Chronicle* of that era was genius at appealing to and exacerbating San Franciscans' propensity toward civic chauvinism. There is no question that the *Chronicle* helped us San Franciscans to identify ourselves and our city.

"A Great City's People Forced to Drink Swill" was one of the famous *Chronicle* headlines of German's era that I remember from when I first started reading what was referred to fondly as the *Chron*, even as it was criticized for its carnival-like antics. The paper slammed San Francisco coffee back in 1963 as "uniformly bad. It is either tasteless and pallid, or it is stale, flat, bitter, rancid, and otherwise noxious." An accompanying editorial called decent coffee "a basic right" and mourned "the shameful manner in which ignorant, money-grubbing, hole-in-corner restaurateurs of San Francisco crudely ravish this beer among brews." Another front-page story, one that hit the streets in 1969, evangelized against a local bakery for changing the packaging of its English muffins. "A bakery blasphemy is abroad in San Francisco," the paper screamed as it informed its readers of another crisis most were unaware that they faced. "Foster's English Muffins are being sold sliced. As everyone here knows, English muffins are never touched by a knife. 'You must tear, tear,' says the San Franciscan to the benighted visitor."[21] This was the type of journalism that fueled the paper's coverage of the State of Jefferson.

It was early in his tenure at the paper that Bill German found himself editing Stanton Delaplane's dispatches from the north. He and I meet in his home in Marin County to talk about those good old days. He starts telling me newspaper legends as soon as we sit down at his cluttered desk: how he saved the paper from joining the *Chicago Tribune* in 1948 with a "Dewey Defeats Truman" headline, and how he was disciplined by his editor when he made up the name of an escaped monkey. A weathered sign on the wall over his desk advertises JOB ORDERS TAKEN HERE/DAILY & WEEKLY/SAN FRANCISCO CHRONICLE/DELIVERED BY CARRIER 15¢ PER WEEK.

A shock of pileated stark-white hair crowns German, matching his brush moustache for a dapper look. He's a little unsteady on his feet, and his hearing loss forces me to interrupt him with almost-yelled questions. But his answers are detailed, vivid, and told as if those long ago, often-comedic adventures experienced by the paper's reporters and editors occurred just yesterday.

"There was some hanky-panky," he tells me when I ask for behind-the-scenes Jefferson stories. "But we dropped it like a hot potato as soon as the first bulletin came in from Pearl Harbor," he says about the series. "Delaplane said these guys [the Jefferson rebels] didn't have any idea of how to sell a story or make up a story." German quickly adds that journalism ethics weren't at issue for the paper or its reporters and editors back in those days. "Delaplane was never above making up anything." German reminisced about "Del" and the dry martinis "which he loved to drink, with one elbow on the bar."

The Jefferson series was the second Pulitzer Prize for the *Chronicle.* "There was no story there really," German tells me about the front page splash the paper gave the Jefferson dispatches. "It was never going to happen," he says about secession. "I knew Delaplane and I knew that whatever he was writing, two-thirds of it probably was stuff he was making up." It won the Pulitzer, German believes, because the prize committee was looking for a story that had nothing to do with the war. The committee said otherwise, noting that it awarded Delaplane the prize "for distinguished reportorial work during the year 1941."

"That winter was a very grim and sad time for America," Bill German remembers. "The Japanese were going to land. We had a blackout every night. It was a lucky thing for the *Chronicle,*" he says about the prize, "and a wonderful thing for Delaplane."

Not that German is necessarily being judgmental when he calls the bulk of Delaplane's Jefferson reporting fiction. "He had a knack," he adds with approval, calling Delaplane's prose "shiny and wonderful" with a tone of voice I'm already beginning to recognize expresses German's droll sense of humor, and which is augmented by an extra sparkle in his eyes. "He said he went up there and these people had no idea of how you promote something. Mayor Gable thought it was a great idea to give out the Proclamation to motorists as they were crossing the border."

I interrupt the retired editor. "You're saying the roadblocks and the Proclamation of Independence were Delaplane's ideas?"

"I can't prove that," he says. "But in interviews, he said that."

German tells me he concocted a headline for one of Delaplane's Jefferson dispatches, a line he still remembers well: "Secession Snowball: 'It's No Joke—We Need Some Good Roads!'" His boss congratulated him and said it would sell a lot of papers. "Made me proud of journalism," he says with what sounds to me like snide irony, adding, "and I knew it was all bullshit. Or I suspected."

The Jefferson dispatches are on his desk as we talk and he reads a line from one aloud. "Gable is the spark plug that is setting this secession world on fire." German looks up from the text, and says about the reporter he was assigned to edit, "He's writing this to goad Gable into doing more."

Delaplane's copy came to German's desk for editing, but he says he didn't touch it. "I just let it go. Once he got a hold of things, his imagination just came to him. He was coming up with brilliant stuff."

"That he made up?"

"He could have. You know, the first language I learned was Yiddish." I now recognize how he answers my questions. He tells long and involved stories with the answer to my question the punch line. "I'd say to my grandmother, 'Tell me a story,' and she'd tell me a story. And I'd ask her a question about it and she'd say, '*Af a mayse fregt men kayn kasha nit.*' If it's a story, don't ask questions. I was probably six or seven years old. It was good advice."

Despite a fertile imagination, German says that when Delaplane was covering serious news stories—a prison riot on Alcatraz, out-of-control San Francisco crowds when World War II ended—the facts prevailed.

Before our meeting ends, German regales me with the escaped monkey story. It happened one day at the World's Fair on Treasure Island in San Francisco Bay, at a time he was looking for a chance to advance from copy boy to reporter. The *Chronicle* office received word that a monkey was loose on the island. "The cops were chasing the monkey," and the editor on duty told German the story was his. "All day the cops were chasing the monkey and I was making up the kinds of things a monkey could do at a world's fair. My role model was Delaplane."

"You were making up the stuff in the story?"

He doesn't answer me. Maybe because of his hearing loss, maybe it's wily obfuscation.

Instead he continues the yarn. "I had to point out to the police where this monkey was hiding. It was hiding behind the guns at the Sally Rand show. The guns were the only things the girls wore below the waist." Sally Rand's Nude Ranch was one of the hits at the fair. "These big guns hid their genitalia. The monkey was hiding behind the guns. That's how they caught him." These years later German still loves the story. "The idea of a renegade, fugitive monkey being caught at the Nude Ranch, I'm thinking it might even get on Page One if I wrote it short and right to the point. So I did. And by God, it didn't make Page One, it made Page Three. But with a byline!"

Before German knew his story was going to be featured in the paper, "a guy named J. Campbell Bruce, who was the city editor, yelled, 'Bill German! Come up to the city desk!' I didn't know what he was going to say."

"He says, 'Did you write this story?'"

"I say, 'Yes.'"

"He says, 'You think it's funny?'"

"I say, 'Well, I was hoping that would come through.'"

"He says, 'It isn't. And I'm going to fix it. You called the monkey Irving. Irving the monkey. You made that up, didn't you?'"

German acknowledged to the boss that he, in fact, made up the name.

"He says, 'That's fine. But no monkey story is ever funny unless you call them Herman.' I remembered this for sixty-two years of journalism," German reports to me about his career influences, "and I never got a chance to write another funny monkey story and call the monkey Herman." We're laughing at a story he's undoubtedly told an endless number of times since 1940, his flat delivery ideal for the tale. "I still think Irving was better," he insists, "but I got a byline and I was happy. What the hell, I had no scruples. I was making the thing up in the spirit of Delaplane." He flashes his cherubic and winning smile, a look that adds to his enigmatic storytelling—it's not always easy to determine when he's kidding and when he's joking on the square (to use slang popular during the *Chronicle*'s heyday). "I had good teachers and good role models." He laughs a laugh that's cartoon-like; it actually sounds like heh-heh-heh—the same exclamation Delaplane used when he laughed about the Ding Dong Daddy telling his fans that he operated trolleys on the "D" line.

Chapter Eight

Liquid Journalism

BACK AT THE SAN FRANCISCO AIRPORT WAITING FOR MY FLIGHT out of town, I stopped off at the airport branch of the Buena Vista Café and stumbled into Stanton Delaplane's reputation once more. Years ago I worked next door to the original Buena Vista, opposite the Hyde Street cable car turntable at the corner of Hyde and Beach Street near San Francisco's Fisherman's Wharf. Plenty of evenings I stopped off at the BV for one of their famous Irish coffees. At the airport the menu reminded me that, as the official story is told, on "a cold and foggy night" in 1952 the owner of the Buena Vista at the time, Jack Koeppler, "challenged international travel writer Stanton Delaplane to help recreate a highly-touted 'Irish coffee' served at Shannon Airport in Ireland. Intrigued, Stan accepted Jack's invitation, and the pair began to experiment immediately. Soon the fame of the Buena Vista's Irish Coffee spread throughout the land. Today, it is still the same delicious mixture."

Indeed it is.

Off comes my sweater as I walk toward Old Sacramento, waiting for the California State Library to open so I can peruse the Stanton Delaplane papers. When I started this stroll at eight in the morning a chilly wind was blowing, but the Sacramento Valley heats up fast in August and triple Fahrenheit digits are forecast for midday. This metropolis, this world-class capital city, is indeed far from sleepy Yreka and sleepier Port Orford. I walk along the Capitol Mall and watch office workers and government bureaucrats—their Starbucks in hands and ID badges around necks—file into glass and steel sky-scrapers or stately neo-classical rockpiles sporting on their facades the Great Seal of the State of California.

California's seal is a more complex collection of symbols than the simple Jefferson double cross. The official interpretation takes us back to Roman mythology. Dominating hillsides and the Sacramento River is Minerva, the Roman goddess of wisdom. Passive at her feet is a griz-zly bear, designed to represent the state's abundant wildlife, despite the fact that farmers, ranchers, gold miners, and thrill seekers relentlessly attacked grizzlies, and the California grizzly—our state animal which also graces our California Republic flag—is extinct.[22]

Publicity stunts and California history are inseparable. Just as the 1941 State of Jefferson movement originated in publicist Gilbert Gable's mayoral office and *Chronicle* reporter Stanton Delaplane's dispatches from Jefferson were front page fodder to help sell papers, so did the *Chronicle's* longtime competitor use a grizzly to draw attention to itself. San Francisco *Examiner* publisher (and private zoo owner) William Randolph Hearst assigned one of his report-ers, Allen Kelly, to bring home a grizzly for the paper in 1889—a time when the grizzlies already were in retreat. The enterprising Kelly found one trapped down in southern California and secured him for "The Chief." Kelly showed his worth as a reporter when he described the restrained animal. "The bear made furious efforts to escape from the trap. He hurled his great bulk against the sides and tried to enlarge every chink that admitted light. Only by unremitting attention with a sharpened stake was he prevented from breaking out."[23] The *Examiner* named the bear Monarch (the paper's motto was "Monarch of the Dailies") and exhibited him to an enthralled readership as California's last grizzly, although he died in 1911, well before the last grizzly on record was shot and killed in 1922.[24] Monarch is exhibited still, stuffed and displayed at the California Academy of Sciences in San Francisco, a memorial to the grizzly slaughter.

Next to Monarch on the state seal is a bunch of grapes, to signify California's abundant agriculture. A miner hoists a pickaxe over expected mineral riches on the riverbank. The bucolic scene is headlined with the Greek word *Eureka:* I have found it. Eureka is the name of the northern California coastal city and Humboldt County seat that lies well within some versions of Jefferson's boundaries.

BRING ME MEN TO MATCH MY MOUNTAINS, reads the legend on one of the state office buildings I pass, the opening line penned by the journalist Sam Walter Foss for his manifest destiny ode, "The Coming American." Its conquering themes make it a candidate for a Jefferson official state poem. Bring me men "whose thought shall pave a highway up to ampler destinies," dreamed Foss in 1894. "Bring me men to match my forests," and "men to match my rivers." Before the final verse he sought men who would clean "the dragon slime of nature." Were we ignorant or arrogant (or both) in that era before Earth Day, carbon credits, and a growing appreciation of the dragon slime of nature?

I cross a bridge above ten lanes of Interstate 5 (over twice as wide as the same highway when it passes through Yreka about 250 miles north of here) and head toward Tower Bridge and the Sacramento River, stroll the wooden sidewalk along the riverbank and look out at the nineteenth-century storefronts preserved in Old Sacramento along with the antiquated passenger cars painted in the livery of the Sacramento Southern Railroad. I check out the stately old Southern Pacific depot, now home to frequent Amtrak trains that run up and down the Central Valley and out along the river to Oakland. I head back toward downtown. The loudspeaker from a streetcar announces to passengers that it's bound for Folsom. Palm trees loll around the glistening white Capitol building, which reminds me this early morning—for some reason—of the presidential palace in Port au Prince, destroyed by the 2010 Haiti earthquake. Maybe I'm thinking of that banana republic, the poorest in the Western Hemisphere, because the headline calling out to me from the *Sacramento Bee* in a sidewalk box on the corner is one more reminder from Governor Jerry Brown that California continues to suffer severe financial woes.

After my Sacramento early morning walkabout, the library's special collections room is open. I'm ushered into the Rare Materials Reading Room. The librarian locks the door behind her as she exits, leaving me alone with the Stanton Delaplane file. I expected to find a trove of Jefferson material: exchanges of letters with his editors, unpublished notes analyzing the Jefferson statehood movement, his role in it and his Pulitzer Prize. But there was nothing much more than photocopies of the Jefferson dispatches and a 1988 letter posted by an avid *Chronicle* reader from Alturas named Les Turner. Turner wanted Delaplane to know that the *Modoc County Record* publisher had responded to a Jefferson statehood commemorative article titled "Will the North Rise Again?" that was published in 1988 in the *Chronicle's* Sunday magazine.

"We are an isolated forgotten corner of the state," the Record's publisher Bob Sloss acknowledged in response to the *Chronicle's* question. He quoted a story from the November 27, 1941, issue of his paper that was written by then-editor R. M. "Gop" Sloss. "Probably the most radical, crack pot idea ever heard of," Gop Sloss wrote. "California has been good to us. We've always gotten our fair share." More than fair, opined Bob Sloss in 1988, explaining to his readers, "The real fact is, residents of Modoc receive more state and federal support on a per capita basis than any other county in the state. Our roads, our schools, our share of government spending is supported on lopsided levels by outside government spending."

Delaplane's correspondent was more prosaic. "I remember most poignantly," wrote Les Turner to the newspaperman, "a column you wrote either in the late forties or early fifties about one of your cats that was killed by your dog over a package of meat you left on top of a refrigerator."

I rang the buzzer and told the librarian I was finished with the Jefferson box. I decided not to bother asking her to retrieve an item in the Delaplane collection that caught my attention for a moment just because it seemed like such an odd thing for the library to choose as a keepsake. It was listed in the catalog simply as "unusual knife." It seems when the Delaplane family donated the collection, the terms of the deal were tough: Take it all or you get nothing; no editing allowed.

Deep in the special collections of the Mill Valley library, Stanton Delaplane himself checks in with details about his Pulitzer-winning escapades in Jefferson. The date is 1978, thirty-seven years after he filed his dispatches from the north country (and ten years before he died at his typewriter: his last *Chronicle* column was published that day). In October of 1978 Delaplane sat for an interview with Mill Valley historian Carl Mosher.

"I began taking charge of it," he told Mosher about the nascent secessionist movement. "I could see they needed a little help." As he talked with Mosher, Delaplane explained how he helped create the breaking story he was covering, calling it "a press agent kind of thing." He called Mayor Gable "a simple, barefoot press agent [who] got himself elected mayor of Port Orford. He was press-agenting it," Delaplane said about Gable's initial calls for secession, "and I was press-agenting it. So we got together in a little cabin in a small town in Oregon."

Carl Mosher interrupted and suggested that the two compared notes that rainy night of talk and drink.

"Compared notes and decided how we would do it," Delaplane agreed. "The only thing the matter with it was he died the next day of a heart attack." The newsman soberly analyzed what happened next. "It made for a very dramatic ending to a seven-day series, and I think that is what impressed the Pulitzer Prize committee." In the grim early days of World War II, the *Chronicle*'s Pulitzer Prize entry offered a break from what my radio colleague, newsman David McQueen, likes to call "the dismal details of the daily downer." The Jefferson secession, explained Delaplane, "was the kind of thing that I think appealed to them—the last frontier, the guys up there packing guns and things like that. It was the right place to be at the right time," he said about his assignment to the story, "which is the most of anybody's business: to be in the right place at the right time."

The legend of the 1941 Jefferson movement is based on the Proclamation of Independence and on the Highway 99 roadblocks. In the interview with Mosher, Delaplane takes full credit for creating the headline-making elements of the news story he was sent to report.

"It was a half-serious thing with them," he said about the local boys he encountered when he arrived in Yreka. "But as soon as they saw their names in the paper, they began to take it very seriously. Before that it was kind of for fun." Delaplane wrote the fellows a script complete with stage directions. "I said, 'Listen, you'd better get out on the highway.' I wrote them a manifesto, and we stopped cars with roadblocks." Note the use of the first person plural pronoun. "Everybody was armed with shotguns and pistols, but very polite. We would hand out the manifesto and say, 'Pass this out down the line.' We'd give them a handful and say, 'Every place you stop for gas, every place you stop for lunch, leave one of these on the counter.' So we were passing along this manifesto which declared our rebellion against Sacramento and Salem." And Delaplane, of course, was generating fabulous and fantastic copy for his stories.

"I wonder," mused historian Carl Mosher, "if lots of movements don't start out more or less like that."

"I believe they probably do," was the considered response from the coconspirator.

⌒

The 1941 "Proclamation of Independence" remains popular throughout Jefferson. The handbills announced:

You are now entering Jefferson the 49th State of the Union.

Jefferson is now in patriotic rebellion against the States of California and Oregon.

This State has seceded from California and Oregon this Thursday, November 27, 1941.

Patriotic Jeffersonians intend to secede each Thursday until further notice.

For the next hundred miles as you drive along Highway 99, you are travelling parallel to the greatest copper belt in the Far West, seventy-five miles west of here.

The United States government needs this vital mineral. But gross neglect by California and Oregon deprives us of necessary roads to bring out copper ore.

If you don't believe this, drive down the Klamath River highway and see for yourself. Take your chains, shovel and dynamite.

Until California and Oregon build a road into the copper country, Jefferson, as a defense-minded Sate, will be forced to rebel each Thursday and act as a separate State.

(Please carry this proclamation with you and pass them out on your way.)

The Proclamation of Independence was signed by the State of Jefferson Citizens Committee, which announced its temporary state capital: Yreka.

Chapter Nine

IS IT A REAL STATE, OR MERELY THE MOCK?

BY NOVEMBER 29, 1941, THE MOTLEY JEFFERSON PLAYERS WHO formed the State of Jefferson Citizens Committee started taking themselves seriously, or so they said in a letter to officials in both Oregon and California, a letter demanding better roads. "Gentlemen you are playing with T.N.T.," they wrote. "And we are serious."[25] The 1938 Cole Porter tune "At Long Last Love," was gaining popularity with a line the Jefferson state backers might well have been singing when they encountered second thoughts about their cause: "Is this a cocktail, this feeling of joy/Or is what I feel the real McCoy?"

When Mayor Gable died he was calling himself "the acting chief executive of the new state" under authority he apparently granted to himself.[26] The leadership void quickly was filled by another self-appointed guardian of the new state, California state senator Randolph Collier. "Gilbert Gable would not want us to falter now," he told anyone who would listen, "after the project he supported so long and so well was near success."[27] Senator Collier and other self-appointed Jefferson movers-and-shakers picked a retired Crescent City judge, John Childs, as their new "governor." Judge Childs was experienced at the role of pseudo-governor. Back in 1935 he had organized leaders of neighboring counties to his own Del Norte who were frustrated by bad roads. They threatened secession from California to draw attention to their complaints.

Senator Collier muses at the Siskiyou County Courthouse.

The 1941 ad hoc State of Jefferson Citizens Committee decided to stage a secession parade through downtown Yreka and a rousing speech by "Governor" Childs at a rally in front of the courthouse. Or perhaps the newsreel crews sent to Jefferson from Hollywood directed the committee to organize the march and rally because their cameras needed the "news." Which came first seems lost to memory and history. Aiding and abetting the carnival atmosphere was the *Siskiyou Daily News* and its coverage of the statehood movement. "Please attend the filming and be photographed," cajoled the newspaper. "Please wear Western clothes if they are available. Parents are urged to bring their children. Two hundred people in western costumes will be selected to march past the cameras for close ups."[28] Hundreds of locals responded to the paper's call. They paraded with torches up Miner Street. They crowded in front of the courthouse to hear their new "governor" speak. Many obeyed the request that they wear western clothes.

When I screen the scratchy old black-and-white remnants of newsreel footage, the parade and rally scenes look like the set of a Hollywood western. In fact, that's what they were. Former California state historian W. N. Davis Jr. called the entire show "a staged production." He cites a newsreel cameraman shouting "Action!" a la Hollywood, followed by specific instructions to the players from the production's director. "Get over there and be looking at the map," the extras are told. A map of Jefferson was posted next to the speakers' platform. "Don't look at the camera!" As the cameras rolled, the orders continued. "Show a little enthusiasm. Wave your arms!" Hollywood knew what it wanted. "When the governor is introduced, throw your hats into the air!"

Despite the silliness on display, the grievances of the isolated counties were real and at least some of the actors began to believe their own secessionist propaganda. "Governor" Childs spoke for them when he concluded his inaugural speech with a rousing, "Yes, we're in earnest about this matter of the State of Jefferson."

The next day the *New York Times* soberly reported the story under the headline, "'49th State' Elects Its Own 'Governor.'" The unnamed *Times* correspondent reported with a Yreka dateline, "Rebellious citizens of the five counties, angered by the failure of the two States to provide good roads and help promote the development of the mineral resources of the region, cheered the new 'Governor' as he delivered his acceptance speech on a platform flanked by a portrait of Thomas Jefferson and a map of the border counties."[29] The article describes a "flag-draped Main Street" and "pistol-belted miners" marching down it, many waving placards with legends that continue to be quoted by Jefferson enthusiasts: OUR ROADS ARE NOT PASSABLE/HARDLY JACKASSABLE and THE LAST FRONTIER/OUR ROADS ARE PAVED WITH PROMISES. With a dramatic flair that the newsreel manipulators could envy, the *Times* story reported, "Mountain horsemen barricaded the main

highways once more to inform"—and here it quoted the "Proclamation of Independence" Stanton Delaplane took credit for writing—that Jefferson was in "patriotic rebellion." The only hint in the
1941 *Times* story that the secession movement was theater comes
in its last sentence, an acknowledgment that the late Mayor Gable
conjured up the whole scheme. "A former New York and Philadelphia explorer and publicity man," reports the paper, "he conceived
the 'secession' movement as a regional advertising stunt."

As the stunt snowballed, Delaplane reported that Jefferson mer-
chants were talking about placing "good road" buckets next to their
cash registers to stash sales tax revenue pennies, which would be
seized by the new state if Oregon and California did not do more for
Jefferson.[30] "'No more copper from Jefferson until Governor Olson
drives over these roads and digs it out of Siskiyou' was the slogan
today," he reported (and penned?).[31] A telegram was dispatched to
Governor Olson. "If California wants copper," it said referring to the
3 percent state sales tax, "they can come up here and dig for it. We
have plenty."[32]

"Governor" Childs embraced—at least in his public speeches—
the notion that Jefferson would be better off without Salem and Sacramento. "The State of Jefferson is the natural division geographically,
topographically and emotionally," he announced. "In many ways it is
a world unto itself," he rhapsodized about his homeland, calling it
"self-sufficient with enough water, fish, wildlife, farm, orchard land,
mineral resources, and gumption to exist on its own."[33] No question
that there was no gumption shortage.

Watching the newsreel footage is great fun. At the side of the
road is a sign delineating the Oregon/California border—it's not
an official highway sign; it's obviously been created for the photo
op. A couple of cars (a sedan and a coupe with the rounded fend-
ers, split windshields, and streamlined look of the late thirties and
early forties) cross in front of the sign. Five men costumed in that

At the 1941 State of Jefferson roadblock *Courtesy Siskiyou County Museum.*

aforementioned western clothing ride their horses toward the sign as two others on foot run into the frame with a rolled up replacement sign that they tack in place reading, of course, STATE OF JEFFERSON. The horsemen dismount and they all cheer the sign, waving their hats and rifles triumphantly over their heads. Next the crew runs over to fetch their blockade. Another sign is staple-gunned in place: STOP/STATE OF JEFFERSON/BORDER PATROL and it's illustrated with the state seal's double cross. Guns are drawn again—pistols and rifles—as a car approaches on cue and is stopped at the barricade. A "Proclamation of Independence" flyer is thrust in the passenger side window and as soon as it's accepted the barricade swings aside. Suspension of disbelief for the viewer is just about impossible as cars speed up to the roadblock and slam on their brakes, the passengers taking the flyers as if such stops were routine, and the barricade swinging open just as soon as they grab the piece of paper.

Trucks spinning their wheels in mud show off the bad roads. The *Siskiyou Daily News* edition with the Headline "Jefferson—49th

State!" rolls off the press. At a Lions Club meeting the front page is held up for the assembled members as is the double cross state seal painted on the gold pan. The crowd applauds. Collier hands the "governor" the state seal, and Childs holds it aloft. Next Judge Childs takes the leash of one of two bears brought to the carnival, Itchy and Scratchy. The newsreel boys must have been thrilled by the bear action.

Cut to the parade up Miner Street. OREGON FORGOT US, reads one sign. DEFENSE NEEDS ROADS, says another. Marchers carry torches, and one holds up a line drawing of Thomas Jefferson. GIVE US ROADS OR ELSE, warns still another sign. There is a corps of uniformed drum majorettes. Mud-splattered flatbed trucks filled with school kids waving still more signs as they ride up Miner Street, V FOR VICTORY/MINERALS FOR DEFENSE/MONEY FOR ROADS. And the sheriff's posse on horseback is the parade's rear guard.

The newsreel shots from the courthouse lawn show a packed crowd, most of the men's heads covered in typical forties-style fedoras. Judge Childs, dapper in a double-breasted suit with his white hair and wire-rimmed glasses, looks the part he's playing: governor. He shakes hands with the other dignitaries, including Senator Randolph Collier, before he makes his rousing inauguration speech.

The black and white footage was never screened in theaters. Pearl Harbor was attacked before the film was processed, reproduced, and distributed. Years later, one of the gun-toting road blockers, Luke "Buffalo Bill" Lange, sat down in the studios of Yreka Community Television to reminisce about those good old days and to add his commentary to the newsreel pictures.

With a cowboy drawl and a deadpan face he explains how bad the Siskiyou County roads were back in 1941. "I was coming out of Butte Valley one time on Red Rock Road. I had a fairly new Chevrolet. Before I got to home all I had was a steering wheel and I was walking down the road. The car had all shook to pieces." But Lange

A motorist (shill or passerby?) studies the 1941 Jefferson proclamation.
Courtesy Siskiyou County Museum

was serious when he recounted that the newsreel reporters orchestrated a reenactment of the original Highway 99 roadblock—they needed the scene for the newsreel cameras. "The news agencies that were here, they picked out the spot themselves. They knew where they wanted to set their cameras up—where the action should be. They told us what to do. They wanted some action. That's why we were jumping around. They said, 'Don't just fool around. We've got to have some action.' We got there early in the morning. We were very excited about it because we had never been on camera, any of us—and to think that we'd have it here in the local movies! They promised us that they'd send us reels and they could show them here in the local theater. But they didn't do it." He debunks the pictures of trucks stuck in the mud as staged for the cameras, suggesting the newsreel producers convinced locals to take water from the adjacent creek to wet the road. Despite the Hollywood treatment, Luke Lange insists it was a "pretty good imitation of the road conditions" at the time in backcountry Jefferson.

Another of the men at the barricades was Dom Favero. I caught up with his son Brian one freezing wintery morning in a shopping center parking lot on the south side of Yreka. Favero was at the wheel of his showroom-perfect 1930 Cabriolet Model A Ford, about to participate in a parade of restored vintage automobiles. He told me his late father was hesitant about blocking Highway 99. But before I sought more details it was impossible not to talk about his bright yellow and black Model A.

"This is a Siskiyou County car," he told me with gushing local Jeffersonian pride. "It was delivered to the Ford dealership in Dunsmuir and sold to a nice lady in Etna." He and his father found it "living behind a chicken coop in Gazelle," a wreck. "The funny thing about it was that the fellow who owned it was driving back to Gazelle with a gallon of gasoline in a glass jug in the rumble seat. The jar flipped over, the gas leaked through the floorboards and caught the whole rear end on fire." When he and his father spotted it, the back end was a charred mess. They offered the owner of the wreck $600 and hauled it back to their place. "We knew that it was a real rare car." Father and son restored it to its just-off-the-assembly-line glory.

"Dad had a gas station in Yreka." Brian Favero was not yet born during the 1941 Jefferson antics, but he knows the family lore—and it's a family that came to Siskiyou County five generations back, for the Gold Rush. "He saw people coming through town who had been stopped at the roadblock. They all had their stories to tell about the guys pushing their weight around as much as they could without getting hauled in by the gendarmes." Dom Favero, says his son, "was kind of a law-abiding fellow, and he thought they really needed to be very careful about how they went about doing this. It had to be sort of tongue-in-cheek because otherwise you were obstructing interstate commerce."

Jefferson is a reoccurring variation on a theme, Brian Favero muses to me from the driver's seat of the Model A. "This part of California doesn't have a big enough voting block to hold any stroke at all in Sacramento. We're like a redheaded stepchild. In those days we got no money for gravel for our roads. Everything was a mud pit up here according to my dad and my uncles and aunts. Today we don't have a voting block big enough to fight the fish wars and the dam wars." He worries that farmers and ranchers ultimately will lose the water they need, and that state agencies too often side with the environmentalists in the fish and dam fights. "We don't have enough wealth up here to be able to tackle this in a court of law, because lawsuits are expensive. As the folks learned with the spotted owl, the only way you can counteract any of this stuff is in a court of law." Yet the region remains dependent on Sacramento for whatever government money is budgeted for the far north of the state. "Yeah, that's true. It's a double-edged sword." He offers an intriguing image. "It's like grabbing cigar smoke. You can't quite get your hands on it."

The Model A shines like a prop on a movie set about Jefferson— it would not look out of place rolling up Miner Street in the 1941 newsreels. "We've always been a rugged individualistic county up here," Favero says, "so when we try to hold our own and we get submarined by the state, it really hurts. We're like Vermont and West Virginia, that part of the world." He cites two regions that did succeed in forming their own new states. He himself looks north when defining his territory to others. "Whenever I go anywhere and people ask me where I'm from I say, 'California,' and then I say, 'Think southern Oregon because we're up there between Redding and Medford and nobody knows that we're there.' People drive up I-5. They know where Redding is. They know where Ashland or Medford is. But they just sort of go into this time warp when they drive across Shasta Valley." He laughs. "It's the damnedest thing."

A former corporate pilot, Favero says he's seen much of the world and nothing beats the beauty he finds at home. "It is stupendous."

Said like a true Jeffersonian.

"Yeah!" he laughs again. "We stick together up here. We wish we could get a little more deference from the state, but we'll just keep limping along and see what happens."

What's happening this morning is a good, old-fashioned, and carefree parade.

Chapter Ten

SACRAMENTO SUBSIDIES

THE 1941 PROTESTS CONTINUING IN JEFFERSON—WHETHER FRIVOLOUS or sincere (or both)—did not go unnoticed in Sacramento. One Fred W. Binks, the chief of the California Department of Finance Division of Budgets and Accounts, drafted a report titled "Fiscal Problems in the New State of Jefferson," which he submitted to his boss on December 4, 1941, the same day Jeffersonians staged their torch-lit parade in Yreka.

The financial picture painted by the economist is not a pretty one. "Independent status for the 'State of Jefferson' would be gained at the cost of luscious fiscal plums now enjoyed by the four California counties participating in this movement," Binks concluded. His specific numbers are stark and question the vociferous complaints from the north country that Sacramento ignored Jefferson. "As a whole, these counties receive approximately $1.32 from the State of California for each dollar paid in State taxes. In addition to this thirty-two cent direct bonus, the California 'Jeffersonians' receive free the multitude of general services provided by their present state government." Binks listed access to higher courts, services of state departments such as Public Health, incarceration of Jefferson criminals in state prisons, and the California Highway Patrol policing Jefferson roads all as representative examples. When he broke down the figures for each country, the balance sheet for Del Norte County ("Governor" Childs's home) made the complaints of abandonment look ridiculous. For each dollar Del Norte sent south to Sacramento, the county enjoyed $2.16 in services.

"All things considered," reiterated Binks, adding what sounds like a taste of urban arrogance, "the 'State of Jefferson' has made a rather good fiscal deal, whether the people there know it or not." The report details several tax options Jefferson could consider to raise the funds needed to replicate services it then received from Sacramento, and argues why none is better than the status quo. "There seems to be only one tax capable of supporting the new State," Binks proclaims from his comfortable California state office building. "If the citizens of Jefferson could place a small tax upon the amusement which the people of California and Oregon are obtaining from their antics, the fiscal problems of the new Commonwealth would be solved for years to come." Fred W. Binks: a bureaucrat with a sense of humor.

There were other naysayers. While the "Proclamation of Independence" was being posted around Jefferson and handed out at the armed roadblocks, something called the Northern Counties Anti-Jefferson Committee reacted with their own handbills and press releases, distributed anonymously in Yreka from a secret basement headquarters in Dunsmuir, a basement that was equipped with a printing press. This opposition argued that the statehood movement was misguided. The secret committee was, in fact, a gang of high school students who decided to attack the Jefferson promoters just for the fun of it. Nonetheless their arguments were added to serious-sounding newspaper accounts of the rebellion. Years later one of the gang exposed their plot. Robert D. Stone, a graduate of the Dunsmuir High School class of 1943, explained that he and his cohorts called off their campaign "due to the fragile nature of pre-1940 automobiles, the price of gasoline (17 cents a gallon), nubile Dunsmuir girls, and homework."[34]

Through all the shenanigans, to use another word of the era, Stanton Delaplane's swashbuckling panache remains credible and indelible. As recently as July 2011, in the *New York Times* story about Riverside County supervisor Jeff Stone talking up his idea to carve a South California out of the Golden State, Delaplane's Jefferson stunts are legitimized once again in the paper's news pages for a new generation. With no hint of skepticism the paper reports, "The closest any campaign came to success was in 1941, when several counties in northern California and southern Oregon campaigned to form the state of Jefferson. At the time, the counties said they did not have enough roads and created a 'Proclamation of Independence.' But just as the movement was gaining traction, Pearl Harbor was attacked and residents put aside their dreams for a new state to work on the war effort."[35]

Yes, that was the official version from "Governor" Childs. He professed statesmanship when he announced that Jefferson statehood was on hold for the duration. "In view of the National emergency," the "governor" proclaimed as his last official statement, "the acting officers of the provisional territory of Jefferson here and now discontinue any and all activities." He claimed that the plot to secede was a success because it drew attention to the region's need for better roads. "We have accomplished that purpose," he declared.[36]

Baloney, Stanton Delaplane told historian Carl Mosher. "They would have dribbled along with it," he said about the Jefferson players and their zeal for the spotlight, "and if it had gone on," he forecast about the escapade, "it would have gone downhill." Walter B. Stafford, the editor of the *Siskiyou Daily News*, agreed. Stafford was responsible for the editorials advocating not just Jefferson but also the street theater that so intrigued the national audience. Yet on December 6, 1941, at a meeting of the amorphous citizens committee, he told his publicity-hungry colleagues it was time to shutter the show. "Next week," he forecast, "someone else's cat will be up a telegraph pole and getting all the publicity."[37]

California state historian W. N. Davis Jr. studied the citizens committee and determined it was a loose amalgam—each member exerted whimsical pseudo authority "speaking his own mind to willing listeners, picked up and added to the 'secession' story. It is true," he wrote in the *California Historical Society Quarterly*, "by the time the movement reached its climax, a few of the promoters had shouted themselves into believing secession would be a good thing if it were constitutionally possible, but the feeling was nowhere widespread, as the press accounts would have one believe."

Chapter Eleven

Smoke and the Iconoclastic Sheriff

It's a smoky day as I head south on Interstate 5 toward my rendezvous with Del Norte County sheriff Dean Wilson, so smoky I cannot see Mt. Shasta where it usually dominates the skyline. Lightning strikes over the last few days started three severe forest fires. Sheriff Wilson operates from his headquarters in Crescent City, hometown of Jefferson's appointed governor, John C. Childs. The car radio reminds me, "It's 8:19 on Jefferson Public Radio," and I listen to the weather forecast for Jefferson: the Oregon coast, Grants Pass, Medford and Ashland, Weed and Mt. Shasta. I leave the freeway at Mt. Shasta where Wilson has been meeting with sheriffs from the other fifty-seven California counties at the Best Western Tree House. He and I meet in the motel coffee shop. The sheriff offers some coffee to me and needs little prodding to talk about what he considers his historic role as—to use what's become such a cliché—an agent of change. Sheriff Wilson doesn't just talk about liberating Jefferson from Sacramento; he lives it.

"I've been on a quest of self-discovery, so to speak, I guess you could say," the life-long lawman tells me as he settles back in his chair, pushing his breakfast plate to the side of the table. It's obvious he's a good eater—his girth reminds me of Buford T. Justice, the *Smokey and the Bandit* sheriff. But unlike the character played by Jackie Gleason in the movie, but Sheriff Wilson is no buffoon being taken advantage of by local miscreants. He was first elected sheriff in 2002

"Constitutional" sheriff Dean Wilson.

after a career as a Crescent City police officer, and as sheriff often found himself down in Sacramento meeting with the governor and state legislators. "Over a good number of years going down there I realized that these people were completely messed up."

With that it was clear to me that the sheriff deserved the reputation my research suggested: He's not just a good eater; he's a good talker. He doesn't hide his feelings or his politics. "Messed up how?" I ask.

"They're trying to ignore it," Wilson says about how most politicians are dealing with California's ongoing fiscal crisis. "They figure if they wait long enough California will recover. They don't have the ability to fix it. They're just lost." He discovered more. "When we elect people we somehow believe in our hearts that they are leaders. But when you go under the Dome," he's referring to the Capitol building in Sacramento, "it's like any other cross section of America. In a crisis you have about 10 or 12 percent of them who will take decisive action, right or wrong. About 10 to 15 percent will freeze and get run over by whatever disaster is in front of them. The bulk of the people will follow. They will look to whoever is leading and move in that direction."

"Or just sit on the couch."

"Yeah," the sheriff acknowledges, but it's clear he's on the stump and would prefer his speech is not interrupted. "They're primarily sheep," he says about most Americans, "and they're just going to go in the direction someone is herding them." That most legislators are not different from those sheep was the epiphany that led to his quest of self-discovery. "Unfortunately there are few true leaders in the Capitol. That was my strong awakening."

Sheriff Wilson—in casual civvies as he talks at the breakfast table—decided that his badge obligated him to take a leadership role. Well over half the jobs in struggling Del Norte County are government jobs: city and county work, the notorious maximum-security state prison at Pelican Bay. Logging and fishing—industries that fed the county for generations—are both exhausted. More government support comes from the subsidies his impoverished constituents receive: food stamps, welfare, and unemployment insurance. He's worried that California's unsolved economic problems mean whatever is left of the social safety net will collapse, with devastating results for Del Norte County. And he's not just worried about shoplifting and bank robberies.

"You have to understand the sheriff's position. The sheriff is the only constitutionally empowered, elected law enforcement officer in the nation." Now we're getting to the self-discovery. "There is no other law enforcement person," he's speaking slowly, his voice soft, but deep and strong, and he's choosing his words carefully, "that is a publicly empowered law enforcement officer. Everybody else is appointed. They are not elected officials." This is a critical distinction for Sheriff Wilson who sees his mandate with a Jeffersonian point of view: He must protect Del Norte citizens from mismanagement, power grabs, and other abuses perpetrated by Sacramento and Washington, DC. As an elected sheriff, he tells me, he's much more than a cop on the beat; he serves as the chief of the executive branch of county government.

"In a broader sense, the role of the sheriff is as a constitutional officer." He's teaching his version of high school civics. "When you take the oath, you swear to the Constitution. So as a constitutional officer we are bound to enforce the doctrine of the Constitution and to make sure that we protect the rights of our citizenry—the people that vote us into office." He reiterates the point using familiar language as if it were from the Constitution, "We protect those rights that they have that are inalienable to them, individual rights. It's for us to protect those rights against the intrusions of government or the intrusions of crime."

In fact, that phrase about rights comes to us from the Declaration of Independence, which states, as we all may remember from those civics classes or elsewhere, "We hold these truths to be self-evident, that all men are created equal, that they are endowed by their Creator with certain unalienable rights . . . ." The Constitution, of course, includes the Bill of Rights, but never identifies those rights as "unalienable" (or inalienable, as the sheriff says— both forms are correct, Sheriff Wilson's and Thomas Jefferson's, but the sheriff understandably uses the more contemporary term).

Sitting in the far corner of the coffee shop, I'm hearing a sheriff explain what he considers to be the sweeping, all-encompassing authority and obligation that he's convinced his badge demands. He's duty bound to protect his folks against anything he perceives as a threat—back to the Declaration again and those unalienable rights—to their life, their liberty, or their pursuit of happiness. It's time to move the talk past the theory and hear some examples.

Laws can be passed by the legislature and signed by the governor that are unconstitutional, the sheriff notes, laws that can infringe on an individual's rights. "It's the duty of the sheriff to make sure that if those things do come down that we do not enforce those kinds of laws that we deem to be unconstitutional."

Whoa! Back to civics class. Isn't it the duty of the judiciary to rule on constitutionality? Not in places like Jefferson, instructs Sheriff Wilson.

"It's not good enough for us to sit by and wait for judicial review. It's not the role of the judiciary," he insists. "That has become a more moderate interpretation." Again he recounts the oath of office that he took, an oath to protect the Constitution, not wait around for judicial review. "We're supposed to defend that Constitution." That includes, according to his interpretation of the law and his job, defending and protecting his constituents against those laws he, as sheriff, deems unconstitutional.

I ask for an example of Dean Wilson taking such an official action as sheriff, and he provides a classic.

"Open carry" rolls off his tongue without hesitation. "California passed legislation to ban open carry. I will not enforce that in my county." He repeats and reinforces the statement. "I will absolutely not enforce the laws against open carry in my county because it's unconstitutional. You cannot infringe upon the rights of the citizens to keep and bear arms."

A decision based on the Second Amendment, I figure.

"Based on the Second Amendment," he confirms. What back in 1941 was essentially a State of Jefferson publicity stunt has morphed in the current era into a de facto secession from the State of California. With no formality other than a brazen rural sheriff, the "sheep under the Dome" are emasculated and the laws passed by the state's elected representatives in Sacramento are ignored.

"If I walk down the street in Del Norte County with a pistol strapped to my hip, see you on the sidewalk and say, 'Good morning, Sheriff,' you say what to me?"

"Good morning. Have a nice day." He laughs.

"And your deputies?"

"Same. They operate under my authority."

"So I would have to violate a law you think is appropriate to enforce before you stop me. If I continue down the street, walk into the bank, pull that pistol out of my belt, and say to the teller, 'Give me all your cash,' and you see me through the bank window, you do what?"

Of course he says he'll arrest me for attempting to rob the bank.

Carrying unloaded exposed guns in public or in vehicles became illegal in California when Governor Jerry Brown signed a bill in 2011 passed by the state legislature that had been introduced by Pasadena assemblyman Anthony Portantino. "Main Street is not the Old West," said Portantino, "and you don't need a gun to buy a cheeseburger."[38] Carrying loaded weapons in public was already illegal in California. It was illegal ever since Governor Ronald Reagan signed the Mumford Act in 1967, announcing there was "no reason why on the street today a citizen should be carrying loaded weapons." The former Hollywood cowboy and future president said the new law "would work no hardship on the honest citizen."[39] Assemblyman Don Mumford authored the legislation Reagan signed, a bill that targeted the Black Panther Party and their then-legal armed neighborhood watch patrols, confrontations orchestrated to observe and influence police practices on the streets of Oakland.

Main Street Pasadena may not be the Old West, but Main Street Crescent City can feel like it, and much of the countryside around Crescent City is little changed from those Old West days. The bulk of Del Norte County, like most of Jefferson, is public land—administered by the state and federal governments. Sheriff Wilson's frustrations include the federal rules and regulations restricting the use of backcountry roads through public territory overseen by the Bureau of Land Management and other government agencies.

I try another scenario with the sheriff.

"I'm at a fence gate locked by the BLM and I get out of my pickup, snap the padlock with my bolt cutters, and head toward my favorite trout stream. You're sitting in your squad car drinking coffee and watching me. What do you do?"

"That's vandalism," he reminds about breaking the lock.

"Let's say the gate is just closed," I amend my tale, "and a sign says, 'This BLM road is closed.' I open the gate and go fishing. You say what?"

"Have at it. The reality is that this is public land."

The sheriff says neither Sacramento nor Washington harass him for his pick-and-choose law enforcement technique.

"Because this is Del Norte County and who cares about you, you're in the middle of nowhere," I offer as explanation for how he gets away with being an activist sheriff, legislating from his police cruiser. He surprises me by agreeing.

"A little bit of it is because we're in the middle of nowhere. But much of this authority that we presumed existed, doesn't really exist." Most public land is not owned by the federal government, he insists. It's owned by the public and just managed by the government, and as sheriff he has sole law enforcement authority over that public land since he is the only law enforcement official elected in Del Norte County.

"I don't hide my politics." I cannot imagine why he finds it necessary to make such a statement after our chat about guns and fences, so I'm not surprised when he tells me with pride that he and his wife founded his local Tea Party. "I would love to see northern California break away from southern California," says Sheriff Wilson. He draws his wish list line for the state of Jefferson and it's basically an urban-rural split with a warm welcome to southern Oregon counties—1941 all over again. He feels underrepresented because the makeup of the California legislature—both the Senate and the Assembly—is based on population. "We cannot be heard over the cries of urban California." San Francisco and L.A. trump the rural counties whenever there is a conflict of interests. Yet the rural counties rely on Sacramento for revenue. No problem, says the sheriff, we've got gold and more in these here hills.

"Two radical ideas change that dichotomy," he says. He believes that the federal government could be forced to turn over the public lands it administers to the new state and the new state would be free to exploit its natural resources, from timber to mineral wealth to the fisheries. "We could create a state that tries to be strongly independent of federal dollars, and based on individual freedom, individual liberty, and individual responsibility."

But what do you do for a living?

"We have everything we need within our county to be a self-sustaining, viable economy," says the local sheriff. Develop Redwood National Park, he insists, to make it a better tourist attraction. Resume logging, he argues, there's plenty of forestland to generate sustainable needed dollars. Nonetheless, as much as he would like to see a politically independent North California state or State of Jefferson, his pragmatic side doubts it will happen. "But do I think the desire for it to happen is there? Oh, absolutely."

After we say goodbye I realize that the very real Sheriff Dean Wilson and the rural sheriff parody Buford T. Justice as played by Jackie Gleason do share another thing in common: Sheriff Justice's trademark commentary: "What we're dealing with here is a complete lack of respect for the law."

Chapter Twelve

Double Crossed

I HEAD NORTH A FEW MILES FROM MT. SHASTA CITY UP I-5 TO CHECK out the Jefferson special collections file in the College of the Siski-yous library in Weed.

My frequent journeys up and down Jefferson's main street—Interstate 5—are meditative. Cruising along the freeway that replaced old Highway 99 is calming for me. There's rarely traffic of conse-quence to fight. The speed limit ranges up to seventy, which means—well, how fast do most of us go in relationship to the posted limit? Which means that the miles click by fast and with little stress. The panorama reinforces the Jefferson anthem's call for "land, lots of land, and the starry sky above." The vistas change from the evergreen-lined grade coming out of Dunsmuir, to monumental Mt. Shasta (when it's not cloud-shrouded or veiled behind forest fire smoke) looming into view just past the turn-off to McCloud, to the lunar-like landscape on the fast stretch from Weed to Yreka, to sweeping miles of mountain-and-valley views on the climb to the Siskiyou pass (the highest place on I-5 between Mexico and Canada), to the slalom down into the Rogue Valley and the sobering back-to-"civilization" ride through Medford's speed trap of urban sprawl en route to Grants Pass. Jeffer-son's miles of I-5 are as familiar to me as any American main street is to its locals—I've been hurtling up and down it regularly since 1973. Radio reception is erratic between Ashland and Dunsmuir. I tend to drive that stretch in silence, keeping the engine's revs up as I climb out of Ashland toward the summit (hoping in winter to make it over the top without succumbing to chains), and then wondering if I forgot some residual forbidden fruits or vegetables as I slow for inspection at the bug station, easing off the gas through Yreka, stopping sometimes between Yreka and Weed for another piece of souvenir volcanic rock, grabbing something seemingly healthy to eat at the Berryvale Grocery in Mt. Shasta, and then careening south down the steep grade toward Dunsmuir. The rumble of the tires on the freeway combines with the wind noise to mesmerize me as if it were a Gregorian chant. My mind ranges from journalism ideas to cosmic questions. The I-5 landscape is one of my cathedrals (my old Volvo bucket seat my pew).

Weed, a lumber mill company town founded in 1897 by entrepreneur Abner Weed, suffered an identity crisis in the early 1970s when some concerned citizens worried that the hometown's image was becoming tarnished. Weed, they feared, conjured images of marijuana in the minds of too many passersby instead of their quaint all-American rural paradise. Mayor Frank Rizzo wanted Weed to be renamed Shastina in order to distance his city from its "relationship to undesirable foliage including marijuana." He argued "nobody likes a weed."[40] The name change was put to a vote, and Abner Weed's memory won. Nonetheless, easily amused tourists stop in town for their Weed souvenirs, keepsakes such as bumper stickers with the slogan MY CHILD IS A WEED HIGH HONOR STUDENT (the words "weed" and "high" are huge, the rest of the text is tiny) and I LOVE WEED printed big with the follow-up IT'S A TOWN, OFFICER, in much smaller type. I looked at The Weed Store on one of my stops for a break along I-5 and checked out the T-shirts decorated with WEED MAKES ME HAPPY in multi-colored pseudo-psychedelic lettering, craftsmanship that makes a not-too-successful attempt at replicating 1960s Fillmore Auditorium and Avalon Ballroom posters. (I am in a position to make the comparison. Sheila and I have an original Family Dog poster framed on the wall at home offering us sage advice: MAY THE BABY JESUS SHUT YOUR MOUTH AND OPEN YOUR MIND.)

Marijuana aficionados do make up another Jefferson constituency that would like to be free of harassment from Sacramento and Salem. The new state would include some of the most productive marijuana-growing landscape in America. The weed farmers with their lucrative cash crop inject big bucks into the Jefferson economy. My research trip itinerary includes a stopover outside Cave Junction, Oregon, in a few days to check out the annual Jefferson State Music Festival Hemp Expo, presented by an organization called Southern Oregon Alternative Medicine and featuring music by the local band which calls itself State of Jefferson.

It was in Weed at the college's library where I found a copy of the "State of Jefferson" typescript, a "musical history lesson" of a play written by Yrekan Gerald Murphy. Murphy researched Jefferson for his script. He corresponded with Stanton Delaplane who, according to Murphy, was proud to take credit for directing the 1941 Jefferson news show, including writing the infamous "Proclamation of Independence."[41] Murphy's musical production ends with the rousing closing lyrics from the title tune. "In the State of Jefferson/Where the wild rivers run/In our mountain land/We will make our stand./Raise the flag and never fear/From Gold Beach to Dunsmuir./We will not be bossed/Never double crossed./Tell them Jefferson is here!"

Hard not to enjoy a tune that rhymes "never fear" with "Dunsmuir." Dunsmuir was first called Pusher, named for the extra engines the Southern Pacific Railroad attached to its long and heavy freight trains in order to get them up and over the Siskiyous. On a trip down from British Columbia in 1886, Canadian coal mining magnate Alexander Dunsmuir took a liking to Pusher and, goes a favorite local story, offered to build a decorative fountain (stocked with trout!) if the locals would change their community's name to his.[42] Alexander Dunsmuir, overseer of the family company's San Francisco office, died of drink in his mid-forties. Had Alexander Dunsmuir not been so vain, Pusher and Weed would be neighbors.[43]

Back on the freeway, I'm speeding toward my next appointment, at the Siskiyou County Museum. The radio reminds me I'm still tuned to Jefferson Public Radio "which you can listen to anywhere in the mythical State of Jefferson." Maybe. As I ramble through the Jefferson countryside studying its status and meeting Jeffersonians, mythical doesn't quite seem like an accurate description. There is a reality to the Jeffersonian sense of identity that does not require official statehood. The hay barn looms on the east side of the road, reminding me again where I am with its huge letters spelling out STATE OF JEFFERSON.

The impossible-to-miss Interstate 5 hay barn.

Yreka old-timer Richard Terwilliger is manning the front desk at the Siskiyou County Museum when I show up for my appointment to study the Jefferson file, the lone visitor to the museum this day. He surprises me by pulling out a cardboard box that's stashed in the reading room where the archives of the Siskiyou Historical Society are housed.

"Want to see the Jefferson seal?" he asks, his eyes expressing pending surprise and sure delight. With his white hair (what's left of it) and his white moustache, he could almost be a candidate to play Santa Claus—he just needs to put on plenty of pounds in order for his belly to shake like a bowl full of jelly.

"One hitch," he says. "You've got to wear white gloves when you handle it." Terwilliger pulls the gloves onto his hands and respectfully removes the gold pan from the box, showing it off to me: the pan painted yellow to signify the gold in the Jefferson mountains and the two black X's as reminders that Jefferson is double crossed by Sacramento and Salem.

The gloved hands of Richard Terwilliger support the Great Seal.

Terwilliger is a Jeffersonian who grew up in the countryside surrounding Yreka. "It's a totally different culture down there," he says about urban California, and he's not happy with the outsiders who move north to Yreka. "They move up here and try to change this country to what they left," he reports, puzzled by the urbanite transplants. "They just want to take over. I tune them out and tell them, 'You should become more like we are, more independent.' It's just common sense."

Richard Terwilliger gently places the gold pan relic back in its box. I collect my notes and head for the door.

"Drive carefully," he cautions me. "Crazy drivers out there."

"Sure are," I nod, and feed him a punch line, "and they're all from southern California."

I'm rewarded with a laugh of agreement.

Chapter Thirteen

The Two State Solution

The contemporary poster boy for splitting California into at least two and maybe three states must be former California assemblyman Stan Statham. I felt as if I had known him for years as soon as I met him because I've known jocular fellows like Stan (with our first e-mail exchange we established ours as a first names Stan & Peter relationship) throughout my broadcasting career—easygoing and good-looking guys, comfortable with their natural ability to communicate and somewhat bemused by their celebrity. Stan Statham started on the air as a radio disc jockey, but soon was presenting the news on television. From that pedestal it was an easy jump to the state legislature. Statham calls himself—I'm convinced mostly in jest—"totally unqualified" for the job his rural northern California district chose him to do, elected only "because I'd been on TV for a half hour at six and eleven for ten years. I mean, not that the public is uninformed, but they like to vote for people with whom they're familiar."

We're sitting in a quiet hotel lobby restaurant in San Francisco while he recounts a common experience from campaigns past. He is a distinguished-looking man, impeccably dressed, his silver tie matching his silver hair. He looks as if he could play a statesman role on TV.

"I met thousands of people and they would just say, 'How are you, Stan? It's a pleasure to meet you.' And then their second sentence would be, 'I had no idea you were this tall.' It was too easy," he says about being elected to office.

Stan "let's split up California" Statham.

In his last term in the Assembly (California's term limit law forced his retirement from the state legislature), Statham became convinced that the state government was dysfunctional. He was aware of at least some of those two hundred or so failed attempts over the years to divide California. The closest any of the campaigns came to success was in 1859 when Los Angeles assemblyman Andres Pico wanted the north and south split at the Tehachapi Mountains just north of L.A. Pico's bill passed both houses of the state legislature and was signed by Governor John Weller. Governor Weller alerted Washington that California wanted to become two states. A bill to do just that was introduced in the House at the same time as the nation was tumbling into the Civil War. Congress did not act further on the California petition; the bill died.[44]

Despite all the years of various failures to carve California up into more than one state, Statham decided to take on the challenge himself. He managed to get a bill out of the Assembly to split the state into three; it was killed in the Senate. Now—no longer in office—he continues to work for a divvied up California. His latest idea is to create a coastal state and an inland state. His political theory is that the coast would elect Democratic senators and the inland Republicans. This would double the region's representation in Congress, but it would be politically palatable: Neither major political party would gain a numerical advantage. Statham is thinking like a politician. He isn't just appealing to the needs and emotions of constituents; he's trying to create a proposal that could find acceptance in Washington and appeal to Sacramento.

"It's just a different culture," this Chico native says about southern California.

We're talking in the Hilton Hotel across from Portsmouth Square, far from tourists crowding downtown hotels around the city's Union Square. The lobby is quiet; a soft player piano is serenading us with standards from the Great American Songbook, things like Cole Porter's wild refrain, "Is it the real turtle soup or merely the mock?" I pull out a yellow legal pad and draw a crude-looking rendition of California and Oregon, marking the boundaries of the 1941 Jefferson.

Statham rejects it. "When I started to divide California twenty years ago," he admits, "I never heard of the State of Jefferson. It's just too difficult," he says about the politics involved in carving the new state out of both Oregon and California. But he believes California is dysfunctional because it is too big, both in land and people. "We've got more people than Canada," he marvels about the thirty-seven million Californians. "Something smaller you can handle," he says, and points to his wife as an example. "This is both of our second marriages," he tells me. "I had two kids. She made a mistake and had four. And it was more difficult." Stan Statham is fast with the one-liners and sometimes it's hard to know when he's joking—as is the case with former *Chronicle* editor Bill German.

When the 1941 Jeffersonians kicked around what to call their new state, the rebels considered Mittelwestcoastia, Orofino, Bonanza, Del Curiskiou, Siscurdelmo, New West, New Hope, Klamath, and Discontent before deciding on Jefferson. Mittelwestcoastia rings just about right for the bizarre continuing history of this elusive new state.

What should the two new states be called? Statham refuses to express his opinion. Not important right now, he insists.

Not true, I parry. "Your name is Stan. If I start calling you Fred, this interview will suffer." But his point is valid.

We create our own identities in part by how we relate to where we call home, and what that home is called can be vital to our sense of place. International crises occur over names. Just ask Greece and the former Yugoslavian republic of Macedonia, or ask Taiwan and Beijing (Peking!) about the name China. That's why what a split-up California would be called is unimportant to Statham. If legislative efforts to cut the state into two include such details, he fears the proposal never will succeed because voters and their representatives will become mired in debate over the name, passionate about what the place(s) will be called. Agree to the split first, he says, then vote for a name or stage a contest.

Like *American Idol*, I suggest, and then ask another question Statham dodges. "Where do we put the extra star in the flag?"

"Everybody is so panicked out about where to put the fifty-first star." He dismisses my query as unimportant.

But like a state's name, the nation's symbols are important. I ask again, "Where do you put it?"

"If you can adjust forty-eight stars or fifty stars or thirteen stars, you can always find a place to put it."

"Have you sat down with a piece of paper and a pencil and doo-dled it out?"

"No, I'm not a very good graphic artist."

"Just in terms of the geometry of the flag's field of stars, where might you put it?"

"Yeah," says Stan Statham, "it's not an even number." He acknowledges the challenging design. "But the result on the ground would be good. The flag is somebody else's problem."

Although Stan Statham dodges the new state name question, the press release he issued in 1991 calling for a county-by-county referendum on splitting the state does quote a likely candidate for namesake. "For 15 years the people I represent in the vast First Assembly District have told me they are tired of the huge, unresponsive, elected and unelected government that has become the state of California," wrote Statham. "I think the time has come to see if this feeling is shared by all of California." Then he quoted one of the nation's most quoted founding fathers. "All authority belongs to the people," said Thomas Jefferson.

Another Jefferson fan was southern California assemblyman Jan Goldsmith, who checked in with one of his favorite Jefferson lines when Statham's state splitting efforts were being debated in 1993. "Jefferson said it is not by the concentration and consolidation of power, but by the distribution of power that good government is effective," was Goldsmith's paraphrase.[45]

Chapter Fourteen

LESS IS MORE

DEFINING OURSELVES BY PLACE IS HUMAN NATURE.

Over cups of tea in the Amman, Jordan, old souk I chatted about the meaning of place with a merchant selling fabric; I bring cloth from foreign ports of call home to my wife for her vast collection. The shopkeeper expressed his appreciation for the Hashemite royal family, giving the king credit for keeping Jordan at peace with its neighbors. Then he explained what's wrong with those neighbors.

"In Lebanon there are too many problems. In Syria you cannot talk. In Iran they shoot you. In Iraq they bomb you." He was enjoying his critique, not thinking about business as he summarized Middle East politics for me. "In Afghanistan they slit your throat. Saudi Arabia I don't like."

When he finished his list I asked, "And Israel?"

He was quiet for a moment before he murmured, "I'm Palestinian. It's very difficult." He stopped talking again before finally asking me a question about my questions. "Are you CIA?"

"No," I tried not to look spooky, "a journalist." Just as bad? I finished my tea, chose some cloth to take home and we shook hands—he probably still wondering about my bona fides.

One of my favorite stories about such parochialism occurred in one of my favorite restaurants in my old California hometown, Fairfax. I told it in my book about another California border—the one on the southern end of the state—*Calexico: True Tales of the*

Borderlands. I am fortunate enough to have lived on and reported from all sorts of borders, political and social. Berlin before the Wall came down. The Greece-Turkey crises. Afghanistan-Pakistan. The Iraq-Jordan line. North and South Korea. I've heard the Montana jokes Minnesotans make. Along any borders cultures exchange with each other and thrive, even as the artificiality of what we call a political border inevitably creates strains. As I was preparing for my trip south to Calexico, I met my friend Markos Kounalakis for lunch in Fairfax, a village on the north side of Marin County, across the Golden Gate Bridge from San Francisco. I had convinced Markos to join me for a week in Calexico. We ate at Fradelizio's ("Ristorante Italiano" it makes clear on its business card, in another example of a drawn border). While we were eating, owner Paul Fradelizio showed up and, as is his style, stopped by our table to say hello.

"How are you?" I asked him.

"Fine, now that I'm back home in Fairfax," was his answer.

The obvious follow-up question was to find out about his travels; it sounded as if he had just returned from distant lands. "Where were you?" I asked.

"San Rafael," he said. "And I always feel so much better as soon as I cross the line."

San Rafael is the county seat, just three miles east of Fairfax. Borders help us define ourselves, and Mr. Fradelizio made it clear he does not identify with San Rafael.

We've been carving up our states since they were colonies. King Charles II gave the land that became Pennsylvania to William Penn in 1681 and he extended his reach to include Delaware. In 1776 Delaware not only signed the Declaration of Independence from the British Empire, it established itself as a state independent from Pennsylvania.[46] In 1764 the Crown gave Vermont to New York and in 1776 Vermonters asked the Continental Congress to admit them to the nascent nation as a separate state. New York objected and Vermont remained tied to its influential neighbor. A year later the tough Vermonters declared their independence from New York, but it wasn't until 1791 that New York relinquished its claim and Vermont became a state. From the time the Revolutionary War began until they joined the Union, Vermonters considered themselves an independent republic—minting their own coins and running their own post office—and it took until 1812 for the two states to agree on the boundary line between them.[47] Maine started wrestling itself away from Massachusetts after the Revolution, but it took until 1820 for it to become part of the Union as a free state, while Missouri joined as a slave state. The Missouri Compromise added the two states without interfering with the nation's balance of free versus slave states. West Virginians chose to remain in the Union when their neighbors seceded and attached their portion of the Old Dominion to the Confederacy.

Almost every state incubates some sort of Jefferson-like separatist movement. Residents of northern Minnesota, northern Wisconsin, and the upper peninsula of Michigan talk of forming a state called Superior. They've been talking about it since the mid-1800s, a sure sign of what Superiorites of Finnish descent call *sisu*, courage and persistence.[48] Although at the Cup of the Day coffee shop in Sault Ste. Marie, proprietor Anthony Stackpole pondered the question former California assemblyman Stan Statham dismissed: "Where are we going to fit another star on the flag?" he wondered.[49]

In the movie *Bernie* (based on a true crime article by Skip Hollandsworth in *Texas Monthly*), a man-on-the-street in Carthage, Texas, describes the borders within Texas. "Carthage is in east Texas," he explains, "and that's totally different than the rest

of Texas, which could be five different states, actually." He's talking over coffee in a diner with trophy deer heads lining the walls.
"You got your west Texas out there with a bunch of flat ranches.
Up north you got them Dallas snobs with their Mercedes. You got
Houston, the Carcinogenic Coast is what I call it, all the way up to
Louisiana. Down south, San Antonio, that's where the Tex meets
the Mex, like the food. And then in central Texas you got the People's Republic of Austin, with a bunch of hairy-legged women and
liberal fruitcakes. Of course I left out the panhandle, and a lot of
people do. But Carthage, this is where the south begins."

The character named Flak in Keith Scribner's novel *The Oregon
Experiment* is an activist associated with "The Pacific Northwest
Secessionist Movement" and preaches, "The best thing we can do
is prepare for the day when the system collapses. No air condition-
ing, people freaking out that they have to sleep on the sidewalk.
They're dying. What we do is get ready. When the power goes down
across this country for good, when the oil and gas spigots run dry,
which will happen, my friends, we'll be eating fresh fruits and vegetables. We'll know how to make our own beer and shoes. We'll
be organized locally. When the U.S. Treasury collapses, when Visa
and American Express and greenback dollars are worthless, we'll
be flush in Douglas dollars."

The granddaddy of Pacific Northwest secessionist literature
must be *Ecotopia*, first published by Ernest Callenbach in 1975. Set
in the year 2000, the premise for the polemic novel remains intriguing: Northern California, Oregon, and Washington secede from the
Union in 1980 and the new nation of Ecotopia seals itself off from
the rest of the States with a North Korea–like vengeance. Newspaperman William Weston is sent by the *Times-Post* to investigate life
in the isolated new nation. What he finds there is an environment-
conscious culture of the type plenty of *Whole Earth Catalog* aficionados longed for in 1975. What makes it fascinating to read today

is that so much of what was a fantasy in 1975 is routine in today's Pacific Northwest, and in Jefferson.

Early during his visit, reporter Weston informs his readers, "Every Ecotopian household is required to compulsively sort all its garbage into compostable and recyclable categories, at what must be an enormous expenditure of personal effort; and expanded fleets of garbage trucks are also needed." While I'm reading that passage the garbage truck is due soon on my street, to be followed by the recycling truck that picks up the paper and metal, and later in the day by the second recycling truck that comes for the glass.

After enjoying his assignment in Ecotopia, our correspondent sends a note to his editor at the paper's headquarters in the States. "I've decided not to come back, Max," he writes. "But thank you for sending me on this assignment, when neither you nor I knew where it might lead. It led me home." Back in the nonfiction world at about the same time the novel was published, a professor at Seattle University, David McClosky, designed a new course he titled "Cascadia: Sociology of the Pacific Northwest." His version of Ecotopia crossed the 49th parallel and included British Columbia.[50] McClosky founded the Cascadia Institute, a think tank that promotes Cascadia and tries to define it. "This movement," writes McClosky, "is a spontaneous emergence arising from the people of the place, a true ecocultural development. It is gratifying to see so many people calling themselves Cascadian and speaking of things Cascadian."[51]

Well before Ecotopia and Cascadia, before Oregon and California, the first white settlers were carving up and naming the Pacific Northwest. By the early 1800s the Hudson's Bay Company was referring to the place as the Columbia District.[52] Thomas Jefferson looked west and saw at the trading post that developed into Astoria, Oregon, "The germ of a great, free, and independent empire on that side of our continent, and that liberty and self-government spreading from that side as well as from this side, will ensure their complete establishment over the whole."[53] It's a quote Jeffersonians of all types like to seize as evidence of their independent heritage (often ignoring the slaughter with guns and disease that their land-grabbing immigrant precursors perpetrated on the vulnerable natives who they encountered during their Manifest Destiny–fueled march west across the American continent).

Chapter Fifteen

NO MONUMENT LAND

IT'S A LONELY DRIVE FROM YREKA TO MY NEXT STOP, SEIAD VALLEY, and to its one store where I've scheduled a chat with the proprietor, Rick Jones. I head east on Highway 96, the Klamath River Highway, one of the roads the 1941 Jefferson revolution used as an example of Sacramento's neglect. Today it's a fine two-lane blacktop, snaking through the canyon alongside the river; the grasses this day are summertime brown. I stop to shoot some photographs. The quiet is compelling: both comforting and eerie. I am alone. There is no other

The Double X banner flying high over the Klamath River in Siskiyou County.

traffic. There is no cell phone service. I was talking to New York City when I rounded a bend miles back and lost the signal. A radio newscaster was reporting a shooting at the Empire State Building and I was checking to make sure family and friends back east were all okay. It's strange how we tend to personalize the news. New York, a city of over eight million, and I'm worried about mine. I couldn't be farther from the New Yorks of the world, here along the quiet Klamath. Here a passing car is a messenger from so-called civilization. Which reminds me of Gandhi's line. Asked what he thought of Western Civilization, the Mahatma reportedly deadpanned, "I think it would be a good idea."

The passing car disappears around a curve and I'm alone again, focusing on my immediate surroundings. I squat down by some weeds and watch a butterfly light, take off, and light again on a different weed. The anxiety I felt when the phone connection was severed relaxes toward serenity. Were I on the crowded sidewalks of New York, it's hard to imagine that I'd be communing with a butterfly. I get back in the Volvo and cascade downriver, watching as the brush and grasslands fill with towering pines. It looks like the set for one of those old Hamm's Beer TV commercials from the land of sky blue waters. I start to notice signs posted along the road demanding NO MONUMENT.

At Quigley's Store in Klamath River (population 150), I stop for water. A huge replica of the Jefferson double cross seal adorns the store's facade. A smiling Ann Hansen is working behind the counter, the half-sleeve tattoo (it's butterflies and flowers!) decorating her bare left arm is fading. I buy a couple of double cross bumper stickers along with a bottle of water and ask Hansen about the NO MONUMENT signs. She is vague about the details, but concerned that if efforts to designate the Klamath River Basin a National Monument are successful, her rural way of life would be threatened. "We like it just the way it is," she tells me, expressing concern about Highway

The facade at Quigley's Store in Klamath River (population 150).

96 becoming a toll road and worrying about water rights. "Congress wants to control us." She likes the freedom to fish and hunt, watch bald eagles and elk. "You can't do this in the city," she tells me.

"What brought you up here?"

"Drive-by shootings and drugs," is her rapid response. "Everybody pretty much knows each other. In the cities hardly anybody knows each other. You're free here. We take care of each other."

"So far!" chimes in a customer who joins us at the counter to buy ice.

"The bluest skies and the most stars you've ever seen," says Ann Hansen as we part.

Twenty-seven more scenic riverside miles to Seiad Valley (approximate population, 350), and the smoke is getting thicker. In Hamburg this sign in a driveway: REAL SHOOTERS DON'T SHOOT YARD BUCKS. One of the out-of-control wilderness land fires is burning just over the ridgeline from Rick Jones's store. He's been a local

Quigley's Store clerk Ann Hansen shows off her butterflies and flowers.

since the late 1980s; like Ann Hansen he's an urban refugee. "The State of Jefferson," he tells me, "is what anybody wants it to be—a state of mind." Jones sells Jefferson T-shirts and Jefferson bumper stickers and Jefferson license plate frames. "It's a tourist trap thing," he claims about his motivation to stock the trinkets. "Anything to make a dime."

We're talking at the Seiad Valley Days annual fundraiser for the volunteer fire department, and the double cross Jefferson flag is flapping on the pole out in front of the firehouse. As smoke drifts down into the valley—it's difficult to see a half a mile— Jones's neighbors are playing horseshoes, eating burgers, waiting for the auction to start. Later in the day the souped up ride 'em lawn mower races are scheduled, along with a barbecue dinner followed by music late into the night.

"They're all crooks," Jones dismisses California's legislators. He's wearing one of the double cross T-shirts he sells for $15 in his store, his pants held up by a pair of bright blue suspenders. "I've always said there ought to be two terms for politicians. One in office and one in jail." He pauses with the timing of a natural comic before he concludes, "And it doesn't matter which comes first." Spoken like a true Jeffersonian.

"All our sales tax money goes south and nothing comes back here," Jones complains.

"Wait a minute," I object. "Studies I've seen indicate Siskiyou County receives more government revenue than it sends to Sacramento and Washington."

"Yeah, it comes back to the county," his response is quick, "and the county spends it in Yreka." It's not just Washington and Sacramento that pose problems for Seiad Valley; county seat Yreka is a villain too.

Kathy Bishop is fixing hamburgers ($5) and cheeseburgers ($5.50) in the back of the firehouse while her husband runs the horseshoe pits out on the side yard. "We're so remote," she says, trying to explain the periodic secession efforts, "and we're not understood."

"Yeah," I acknowledge. "But you've got nothing up here but wilderness."

"Well, that's true," she agrees with good humor. But she's not sure Jefferson needs what it gets from Salem and Sacramento. "We could probably get by with a lot less, though. We're pretty independent."

The auctioneer climbs up on an impromptu stage, grabs a microphone, and taunts the crowd to open their wallets and support the fire department. Rick Jones swigs from a can of Budweiser as he wins a big framed picture of Bigfoot with a $40 bid and announces that it's going up on the wall in his store.

"Next item," announces the auctioneer, "is sugar cookies wearing women's lingerie!"

"Show 'em over here," yells out a guy sitting near the stage with his buddies.

The cookies sell fast and the auctioneer promises to the voyeurs who didn't bid, "I'll pass them around to the guys so they can see what they missed."

Jones buys a full-sized quilt featuring the Jefferson flag. I wander out into the yard and check out the craft booths selling jewelry, wooden toys, greeting cards, plants, and photographs. A chicken and its keeper are standing by a pen with twenty-four numbered squares on its floor. They're waiting for gamblers. The game is called "Chicken Poop Bingo."

Jones loads his truck with his auction haul and we drive the hundred yards or so, past his neighbor's trailer park, over to his store. The Jefferson flag is flying high. U.S. POST OFFICE STATE OF JEFFERSON is painted on the outside wall. Jones looks up at the smoke and fire and mutters, "It's blown up again." A bucket brigade worked by helicopters is making a continuing circuit, scooping water up from the river and flying it to the ridgeline where it's dumped on the spreading flames. The ballet of air and ground attacks on the fire is an example of federal, state, and local government at work together—tax dollars being spent to preserve the forestland and protect Seiad Valley homes. Jones looks up at the fire on another trip out to his truck. "It's jumped the line," he reports to other onlookers.

Jones opens his store safe and retrieves an out-of-print book for me to look at, *Seiad Valley Tales and Tailings: Its Pioneers and the Yreka Gold Dredging Company*, written by the late Brain Helsaple, the fellow responsible for painting the State of Jefferson announcement on the hay barn south of Yreka. An example in the book speaks to Jones's frustrations with "rules and regulations passed in Sacramento that have no bearing on what we've got going here."

"When each and every home in the entire state of California that has an encroachment on a state highway is sold," Helsaple wrote, "the buyer must notify the Department of Transportation to reapply for the encroachment. The driveway is then inspected and must be brought up to current highway standards. The 'double cross' continues." The Klamath River Highway is a state highway and it's the access route for plenty of Seiad Valley homes. Jones is among the Jeffersonians who see the driveway rules and regulations as an unnecessary intrusion on a rural lifestyle misunderstood "under the Dome."

Controversy over gold dredging in the Klamath is another Jefferson conflict. It's a much more inflamed issue than bureaucratic requirements regarding driveways connecting to highways. Unlike disputes between Jeffersonians and Sacramento or Salem, dredging for gold pits neighbor against neighbor, Jeffersonian against Jeffersonian.

Environmentalists and Indians say the dredging destroys fish habitat. "In reality it does not," insists Rick Jones. "In reality a dredge is a big vacuum cleaner. It vacuums all the heavy metal out of the river—gold, mercury, lead—that's been accumulating over the years. It provides deep cool holes for the salmon and steelhead to lie in when the water gets low." He says his gut feeling is that gold dredging has nothing to do with reduced salmon runs.

A gold dredging ban is in effect on the Klamath while we talk.

In the summer of 2012, the US 9th Circuit Court of Appeals ruled in favor of a lawsuit filed by the Karuk tribe in an effort to protect salmon from dredgers. The Indians disagree with Jones's gut feeling and insist dredging the Klamath harms coho salmon habitat. Their suit contended that dredging permits issued by the US Forest Service violated the Endangered Species Act. The court decision overturned lower court rulings in favor of the miners and reflected the acrimony in Jefferson. The judges split seven to four, with the majority insisting that the Forest Service violated federal law by issuing mining permits without consulting those government scientific agencies charged with protecting the coho—which has been listed as a threatened species since 1997. The four dissenting judges sided with the miners and noted that the 3,500 or so permits issued to California dredgers reflected consequential income for the gold prospectors out on the river. Dissenting judge Milan Smith Jr. complained that the ruling "effectively shuts down the entire suction dredge mining industry in the states within our jurisdiction." The ruling covered suction dredge mining in the nine western states in the 9th Circuit's jurisdiction. Expressing what sounds like worry about his court's reputation as much as concern for miners' pocketbooks, Smith forecast that "miners will simply give up, and curse the 9th Circuit."[54]

Suction dredging on the California side of Jefferson had been temporarily banned since 2009 when Governor Arnold Schwarzenegger signed a law requiring that the California Department of Fish and Game conduct an environmental review of the practice and then draft new regulations. Other types of gold mining in the Klamath, those that do not unduly disturb the river's banks and bed or molest salmon redds, remain legal.[55] That includes panning, the process of rinsing river gravel with river water—with a pan like the one used for the Jefferson state seal—in hopes that heavier-than-gravel gold will collect at the bottom of the pan.

Limited legal suction dredging on the Rogue River in Oregon continued after the court's decision, but by Autumn 2012 a coalition of environmental groups sued the US Forest Service, charging that the dredging permits on the Rogue—also coho habitat—should be banned under the terms of the 9th Circuit Court's decision in the Klamath case. "If the Forest Service is going to say 'mine here' or 'don't mine here,' they have to follow the requirements of the Endangered Species Act," said one of the plaintiffs, conservationist George Sexton, when the suit was filed. A meeting with the Ashland-based environmental activist is on my itinerary. "I think it's a values clash," Sexton said about the gold versus salmon debate. "It comes down to what people value public lands for."[56]

Rick Jones says he remembers record salmon runs a few years back during the time suction dredging was allowed. He blames gill netting by Indians at the mouth of the river and the sea lions feeding

Rick Jones, working the bar at the Seiad Valley Volunteer Fire Department fundraiser.

at the mouth of the river for any lack of salmon. Native Americans enjoy special rights to take salmon from the river based on their status as people indigenous to the Klamath Basin.

I play the role of naïve outsider and suggest all the stakeholders talk out the various conflicts of interest in Jefferson and seek compromise.

"There have been multiple meetings," Jones sounds resigned, "and it just becomes a scream-fest." If there were a State of Jefferson—if those distant government agencies were not interfering—Rick figures compromises might be found, locals talking with locals could find solutions to their various disputes, agreements that would benefit the Indian tribes, the gold miners, and the businesses. "I've lost probably 30 percent of my business without the miners," he tells me. "The trailer park has probably lost 75 to 80 percent of his business." Many of the gold dredgers were hobbyists, retirees who bring their trailers and gold lust to the Klamath. "They also buy food, they also buy sodas," says Jones, his voice expressing irritation with the ban. "They do support the economy real well when they're here."

No question the Jefferson economy is a tough one. The unemployment rate is high and businesses are shuttered. Jones's general store is down to two employees from four, he says, and he works about sixty-five hours a week. Yet he's quick to smile when a customer comes through the door. "You have to. What else are you going to do, cry?"

Right on cue the next customer in the door is a frustrated former Klamath gold miner. Hershel "H" Chapman's leathery face shows the deep, dark tan of a perpetual outdoorsman. "There's more gold around here than any other place I've been," he explains his fascination with Jefferson. When I ask him about the dredging ban the response is far from the elegant and measured responses I've heard from storekeeper Rick Jones. "It makes no sense to me. All the heavy metal stays in our sluice box. Not a bit jumps out. We're trapping all the heavy metal." He speaks with a clipped staccato voice.

"What about the fish?" I ask.

"What about 'em? I dug twenty holes one year and I seen a coho in every hole laying eggs. You know what? Before the ban even started, them Indians were on the river screaming and hollering, 'This is my river, get out of my river.' They're idiots."

"H" heads out of the store and I say to Jones, "He sure doesn't edit himself."

"None of them will," says Jones. "Wait until I introduce you to Bruce." Bruce Johnson owns the all-but-empty Mid River RV Park. I look at the forlorn vacant trailer spaces as we drive back through the smoke to the firehouse.

Chapter Sixteen

THE VACANT TRAILER PARK

"YOU WANT TO STIR UP A HORNET'S NEST, HUH?" BRUCE JOHNSON says with a caustic-sounding laugh when Rick introduces me as a journalist studying Jefferson. He's relaxing with a plastic cup full of beer, hanging out near the chicken poop bingo parlor's spot.

"They're here," I say about the conflicts along the Klamath. "I'm stirring up nothing." I refuse to allow newsmakers to blame us messengers.

One of his neighbors interrupts us just as we start talking to inform Johnson of a lifestyle change. "I've swapped the beer for vodka," he says, "It's not as fattening."

"It's faster, too," I offer as commentary.

"Way faster," agrees the celebrant, who wanders off.

I turn back to Johnson and ask him about the Karuk biologist at the Tribal Reunion up at Happy Camp. This weekend Jefferson is celebrating Seiad Valley Days (to raise money for the volunteer fire department), the annual Karuk Tribal Reunion (featuring salmon and acorn soup), and the Jefferson State HempFest (where "cannabis advocates educate the public"). It's a trifecta of Jefferson's often-conflicting interests. The Karuk biologist is manning a booth packed with information about the status of Klamath River salmon, explaining how gold dredging is destroying coho habitat, I tell Bruce.

"I know exactly what they're saying. He's a lying son-of-a-bitch, is what he is," Johnson barks without hesitation, language that seems at odds with his happy-go-lucky banter around the firehouse and his warm smile. Bruce Johnson is a stocky guy. That build, combined with his graying curly hair and beard, give him the look of a man who can take care of himself alone in the woods. His T-shirt reads THE INVINCIBLE IRON MAN and shows off an image of the Marvel Comics character.

Johnson takes a breath when I ask him to explain his point of view, and for now controls his venom. "They kill the fish continuously," he says, referring to the salmon fishing the Klamath tribes are permitted to do with nets down river from Seiad Valley. "These exact same people are the ones who are saying dredgers are killing fish. They cannot demonstrate and they cannot prove that any salmon or salmonoid has ever been harmed or killed by dredging." His speech is fast and precise as his passion builds. "These bastards go out with their nets and they kill them left and right and they say, 'There's a problem, there's a problem.' The biggest problem that you face in this community is the Karuk tribe and the Karuk tribal leadership. You can use my name on this," he says, his facial expression hardening, his voice intense and insistent. "I'm tired of these sons-of-bitches. They've cost me a hundred thousand dollars because they're lying rat fuckers."

The dredging ban, Bruce Johnson is telling me, destroyed his business. But he's convinced the Karuk and other Klamath tribes seek more than an end to gold mining in the river.

"They shut it down," he says, "and they're a bunch of racists." He quotes from what he says was a Karuk website no longer active that the tribe claimed it intended "to use the coho salmon on the Upper Klamath River to drive every white face out of the Klamath River Basin."

He takes another breath.

"I'm going to lose my house. I'm going to lose my business. I'm going to lose everything." He blames the Karuks, and addresses them directly. "There's a reason you guys were considered the scumbags by the rest of the other tribes around here."

His livelihood depends, of course, on the local economy. Most logging is history. Fishing is tightly restricted. Gold dredging is banned. Johnson says his business cannot survive without support from those traditional Jefferson activities: logging, fishing, and mining.

"I grew up in Washington State," his voice softens as he tries to put what sounds like his own racism into context. "I've been around tribes. You know, they're people. These are just dudes. I played football at a Division I level. I don't give a rat's ass what color you are if you can help me win. You're either in my way or you're out of my way. You know what I mean? That's the way life is. It doesn't make any difference what color your skin is, where you go to worship or if you worship at all. I don't care about that. What I care about," and he returns to the dredging ban, "is that what you're doing is damaging me. You're causing me direct harm, and you think that it's appropriate because what you're saying is that you value fish over me. The simple fact of the matter is, whether you like it or not, human beings are still part of our environment."

"Of course we are." I give him a chance to catch his breath. "But one of the reasons visitors want to stay at your trailer park is because there are fish in the river, because the mountainsides are covered with these lovely pines or they want to lie in the sun, not just to dredge for gold, right? This place attracts tourists because it looks pristine."

He's ready with a comeback; he's wound-up again. "This is not an either/or proposition. The eco-movement and tribes want to make it an either/or: If you have the dredging then you can't have the salmon. And it's straight horseshit. I would be willing to put any person in the universe down with me on a suction dredge and within an hour you're going to have a hundred fish around you. All you're doing is releasing biomass. You're not doing anything that doesn't happen every single spring. You pick up dirt, you move it twenty feet, and you put it back."

"Aren't you disturbing the spawning grounds when you pick that dirt up?" I'm querying Johnson with the claims of environmentalists and the tribe biologist.

"No," he insists. "Two specific reasons why. The spawning grounds are not where you're looking for gold. That's what people don't understand." His tone changes from strident to professorial. "When salmon are spawning, they're looking for relatively shallow water—maybe sixteen to eighteen inches deep, highly oxygenated flowing over a broken bed so the eggs have a quick chance to gestate and grow. Where I'm looking for gold is in low-pressure areas, the places that don't have highly oxygenated water because it's deeper and it's slower." Gold, he lectures, is "really heavy. I mean," he emphasizes, "it's *really* heavy. You look at the average rocks in the river and it's like six times heavier than that. It's about twice as heavy as lead." Because of its weight, he explains, it doesn't tend to share the shallows where the salmon spawn. Instead the gold collects in deep pools. He agrees with what his buddy Rick Jones told me back at the store, that the dredging creates clean pools in the river, but not pools the salmon choose for their spawn.

There is no conflict between the mining and the fishery he insists, a conclusion he sums up with Jeffersonian wisdom: "It's apples and basketballs we're talking about here."

But that's not all. Businessman Bruce Johnson is unimpressed with the tribal claims that the coho play a traditional role both in their native culture and in the ecology of the Upper Klamath. He believes the stories he's been told that the coho were transplanted upriver in the early 1900s. "The dredging is being shut down for an invasive species. The coho salmon never made it up past the Trinity River. The only reason it sustained itself is because of the hatcheries

Iron Man Bruce Johnson. (Jefferson's Double X flies beneath Old Glory behind him.)

and the largesse of humanity." Most seasons the Upper Klamath gets too hot for salmon to thrive on their own, he says, competing with the noise of firefighting helicopter rotors beating the air over the river just across the highway. "It's a flat-out lie that mining is destroying the salmon run on this river."

Bruce Johnson flashes an endearing smile between his diatribes and his tone softens again as he talks about his own relationship to the river. "This is the thing that destroys me. If I thought I was doing a second's harm to the salmon," he interrupts himself. "I grew up catching salmon. It's part of my life."

I inject again that naïve idea of an outsider to the river wars. "Why not sit down with your Karuk counterpart," I suggest, "and talk about your differences. Share a beer and another beer, and seek some compromises. Is that a possibility?"

"No," he says without hesitation, "and I'll tell you why. There's all kinds of room on my side. But from his side, the only way we can have this conversation is if I'm willing to give up dredging because he believes it's an either/or proposition." Bruce summarizes what he's convinced his Karuk debate partner would insist. If there are people mining on this river then the salmon will be dead. "That," Bruce tells me, "is simply factually inaccurate and he knows it."

Salmon are a renewable resource, Johnson tells me, a conclusion he says he arrives at from experience. "I commercially fished for years. I've fed people. I've earned money. I've fed myself and my family. Those fish didn't reproduce, but their brothers and sisters did. It's a continuous resource. You're looking at a pasture out here. You can mow the hay and you can retrieve it again. As long as you don't kill the stock, it'll always be there. His position," Johnson tells me about the Karuk, "is that I'm killing the stock and I'm a vile individual for doing it. The fact is that that's not true and he well knows that."

"But if you don't talk it out, what's going to happen here?" I ask, unprepared for his quick answer.

"I'll tell you what's going to happen." His voice is inflamed again. "He's going to bleed. He's going to bleed. It's very close to that already."

"What do you mean by he's going to bleed?" I'm not sure if it's a literal or figurative forecast.

"He's going to get hurt. He's going to say the wrong thing to the wrong person and they're going to take offense at it and he's going to pay for it."

"Physically?"

"Physically. Yes, I'm saying physically. I think it's a lot closer to bloodshed than anybody in the city ever contemplates. I think that the people in the cities have overrun the people in the country. I fell for the first spotted owl bullshit. I get the game. I'm all for ecology. I think if humanity takes a single species off the face of the planet and has the ability not to do it we've made an extremely foolish choice that could someday come back to haunt us in ways that we can't even possibly conceptualize today." Nonetheless he believes the Karuk who are opposed to gold dredging such as the debate opponent I proposed to him "do not consider human beings part of our environment any longer. They consider somebody like me who lives out here to be somebody who's in the way of protecting the rest of the world from people like me. They think that I come out here to do damage instead of coming out here because I love it out here." He stretches out the word "love" as he says it. "I don't want to damage. I want to be able to survive and to work and to make money and to live."

Trailer park owner Bruce Johnson is speaking so fast that the words tumble from him—this combination of profanity, threat, thoughtful analysis, and glib one-liners. "Right now, because of these people's thought process, the number one export from this county is children. There's no work around here. You can't cut down a tree. You can't walk through the hillside. You can't catch a fish on the river. You can't mine it. There're no jobs here for the children. They leave, there's nothing here for them."

"You're painting a terrible picture."

"I know it."

"Is there an alternative scenario?"

"My alternative is to close my business, lose everything, and leave the state before I go to prison. I'm that angry with these people."

Chapter Seventeen

CALMER VOICES

CALMER AND MORE JUDICIAL WITH THEIR LANGUAGE USE THAN Bruce Johnson are two Seiad Valley old-timers I meet with before I leave the firehouse grounds.

"I'm told you're the right guy to talk to about Jefferson," I say to Ed Prather, who interrupts me with backcountry modesty and a soft-spoken, "I'm not so sure about that." Depends on the questions, this World War II veteran and retired telecommunications industry worker points out with a smile.

"We're legislatively poor up here," he explains when I ask about the genesis of Jefferson, adding his voice to the chorus calling the north state disenfranchised from Sacramento. "The high population areas have the representation." But those high population areas lack a resource critical to California's survival. "We've got the water. They don't. But they have the legislative ability to work us over, and it's still going on today."

I ask for an example and he responds with a rural metaphor.

"The slow vine-like creeping of state agencies like the California Fish and Game Commission and the California Water Resources Control Board. Of course there are federal agencies we've got problems with, but that's hardly the question here." Combat one oppressive government at a time. Water greed motivates power grabs from the south, he says, and the state government has all the clout. "I don't know how they're going to solve their water problems down in the

Valley," he says about California's breadbasket. Not that Prather worships the coho and wants to restrict use of the Klamath for the sake of the fish. "I'm not a great advocate of trying to preserve endangered species." He speaks slowly, choosing his words carefully. "These fellows have been working at this religious thought that you can bring back a specie. The coho salmon cannot be brought back," he says definitely. "It has been proven for many years, and it is not indigenous to the area. The Fish and Game Commission introduced it and now they refuse to read the history. It's causing a lot of angst in the community," he says of the efforts to keep coho in the Upper Klamath. "They have to back off."

The helicopters continue collecting buckets full of river. We watch them fly up to the flames and smoke to dump the water on the out-of-control fire as it continues its spread toward Seiad Valley homes and businesses. Ed Prather points to the firefighting operation as another example of outsiders causing him and his neighbors unnecessary trauma. If the Klamath River Basin is designated a National Monument, he claims, such firefighting would be history. Lightning-caused fires like the one we're experiencing would be allowed to burn themselves out. He fears that the National Monument campaign is a land grab and that the ultimate goal of its backers is to take control of all the private property on the Seiad Valley side of the river, to allow transfers of property only to the federal government at prices set by the federal government. But he's an honest interlocutor. "I don't know if that's true or not. I haven't read the bill and I don't know what it says."

There is no bill. National Monuments are designated by a presidential order, usually after the White House receives a recommendation from the Interior Department. According to the Interior

Department, as Ed Prather and I talk, no such recommendation is pending.

I thank Prather for his time and he ambles off saying, "I'll go back and finish feeding my animals."

~

"I was only about ten years old at the time." Retired Bureau of Reclamation irrigation engineer Glen Briggs is thinking back wistfully to the 1941 State of Jefferson escapades. "I'd like to see a separate state," he muses with enthusiasm about such independence. "I don't think we have anything in common with southern California and northern Oregon." But pragmatism intrudes. "I doubt it will ever get anyplace except for the spirit. But I think it would be good."

"So many of those I speak with agree with you that it's a good idea," I report to him, "but then quickly add that it will never get anyplace. What's the holdup?"

"Politics," he agrees with Ed Prather. "Southern California has probably about 80 percent or better of the population and they are not going to lose the natural resources that we have here in northern California. The same with Oregon. The biggest part of the population lives in the Portland area, and they would not want to lose what they have in the southern part."

"But you in the wilderness would be losers, too," I counter. "Sacramento and Salem send you truckloads of goods and services."

He's quiet for a moment before acquiescing, "It would be difficult. But I'm not sure that it couldn't be achieved. We would not be a rich state, that's for sure, except for the natural resources. And with the restrictions on natural resources it would be difficult to be economically viable." Federal limits on logging, fishing, and water use would trump some efforts by Jefferson to exploit the territory. But ridding the region of California and Oregon authority would

provide some relief, he believes, from stifling environmental regulations that are not compatible with Jefferson's wide open spaces. He's
not worried about the type of past rapacious exploitation that over-
fished, clear-cut the forests, and diverted too much water for farming. "I think people and companies would realize that their operation
would depend on continuation of our natural resources."

A woman walks by holding a pie and trips on the uneven firehouse grounds.

"Watch out!" cautions Briggs.

She catches herself and we trade images of her facedown in the
pie before continuing our civics class.

"Do you consider yourself a Jeffersonian?" I ask.

"Of course," he says, as if it's a silly question.

Chapter Eighteen

INDIAN COUNTRY

I LEAVE SMOKY SEIAD VALLEY AND CONTINUE TWENTY LONELY winding miles on Highway 96 to the headquarters of the Karuk tribe, and the old mining and logging crossroads of Happy Camp.

Happy Camp, at first glance, defies its name. It is a desolate-looking and dilapidated place suffering from the same type of deferred maintenance and shuttered businesses as Port Orford. It draws outdoors types for hunting and fishing trips, along with Bigfoot seekers. A towering Sasquatch statue stands guard over the crossroads of the Bigfoot and Jefferson Scenic Byways in the heart of little Happy Camp, population just over a thousand.

I stop at the tribe's headquarters to ask for directions to the annual Karuk Tribal Reunion. The museum store is empty save for the clerk, who sends me to River Park and the *káruk tá kun-yíchaachha*, the people gather together.

"Are you Karuk?" I ask him, always looking for potential sources.

"No," he answers, "German."

"*Sprichst du deutsch*?" The question comes automatically after living for over two years in Berlin.

"No," he says, and then laughs and corrects himself. "*Nein*."

At River Park I get out of the old Volvo and am greeted with outdoor speakers blasting "Hotel California." The song's closing line about checking out but never leaving seems to both transcend and reinforce Jefferson's culture clashes. The reunion program promises "informative booths" and dinner of acorn soup and "traditionally cooked" salmon. "Be sure to let your ELDERS BE SERVED FIRST AT DINNER!" the program demands. A dozen chattering poker players circle a table, bicycles are being raffled, there is a cotton candy machine at work, and bread for "Indian tacos" is frying. I say hello to two Karuk women, one leaning against a tree and the other lying on a blanket. They've displayed necklaces for sale on the blanket and while they wait for customers each is reading (fantasy novels they tell me) on e-readers.

"Don't you miss the ink on paper?" I ask.

"No," they both answer.

"You're abandoning five hundred years of printing traditions. Gutenberg is spinning in his grave."

One of them refers to their beads-and-shells jewelry. "We're combining traditional and contemporary!"

At one booth a young woman is campaigning for Bigfoot Queen. At another I find Ken Brink trying to protect his posters of fish and mussels from the gusty wind. He tells me the gold dredging doesn't just wreck salmon spawning grounds, it also destroys mussel habitat.

"The mussels are in the sediment, the same places they're finding the gold. As they're digging up the gravel looking for gold, they're actually digging up these mussel beds." Ken Brink is Karuk and a biologist working for the tribe's Department of Natural Resources. He considers the mussels crucial components of the Klamath ecology. "The mussels are able to filter one liter of water per hour per mussel." That may not sound like much, but he says each mussel bed can house as many as twenty thousand mussels. "Twenty thousand liters of water are being filtered right there in that spot every hour. Think about how dirty the river would be without these mussels."

"How do you balance value?" I ask. "Is the filtered water more precious than the sparkling gold?"

Karuk biologist Ken Brink, whose shirt informs, "I've come back to my native place."

He answers with a question. "Do we want to start making another species go extinct over gold? Is gold worth the existence of a living species?" He is an intense, fast-talking advocate, a hefty man wearing a gray tank top emblazoned with the words "I've come back to my native place" in Karuk. Sunglasses parked on his head, Ken Brink's smile and eyes radiate a warm personality, a look similar to the welcome I received from trailer park owner Bruce Johnson. "From a tribal perspective, gold is great. Money makes the world go round. We understand that. But the creator put these species here on this earth for a reason. They're supposed to be here. These small mussels may be the keystone species to the whole ecosystem. Maybe if you take away one little part of the system, we're going to have a big collapse. We don't know if the mussels go away what condition the river is going to be in. The river could become so toxic that gold miners might not be able to be in it because of the toxic algae levels that these little creatures help excrete out."

His sales pitch is emotive and heartfelt. He and his counterpart Bruce Johnson perform as if they were trained in the same acting school. They could make ideal partners were they not working different sides of the street. I ask tribal biologist Ken Brink what I asked trailer park owner Bruce Johnson. Why not sit down for a beer with your nemesis and seek common ground, find a compromise. It's that naïve outsider's question again.

His voice slows. "The dredgers and the tribes have big issues. We got the credit— basically the blame—for stopping suction dredging. We have people harassing us every day, saying we took away their livelihood." But he questions the validity of such claims. "A lot of these people who come around dredging are older retired people. They're just doing it for their hobby. These guys already lived their life," he dismisses their role on the river. "They're just trying to find a hobby to make money." With the price of gold at record heights, there *is* money to be made on the river. But for Brink, the dredging must be seen with historical perspective. "Whole mountains have gone," he says about the effects of the commercial hydraulic mining companies that worked the river during the nineteenth-century Gold Rush. "They strip-mined the river so bad that we're still having the effects of heavy metals from the dredgers when they pick up mercury pockets."

Vast quantities of mercury were used by the nineteenth-century miners. Mercury binds readily with gold, making it relatively easy to extract the precious metal as it slips from ore aided by its partner, the deadly quicksilver. Today's miners say they help clean the river when their dredges suck up a mercury pocket. But their opponents counter that not all the newly stirred up mercury—not to mention other toxic compounds from past mining operations—is captured.

"It's hard, man," Ken says when I again suggest he and his colleagues try talking with the miners and their supporters. But he sees room for compromise. Instead of a total suction dredging ban, just don't dredge when the salmon spawn. "It digs up the spawning bed and creates tailing piles that are not stable enough for salmon. It's really loose and the first high water blows it out." Miners stirring up the water with their machines "disturb the fish after they've had this great tribulation from the ocean to here to spawn."

Ken Brink calls salmon the best food in the world. "I grew up a traditional fisherman. My people used to eat a lot of fish." Damage to the fishery forced them to buy store-bought food, he tells me. "Now we have diabetes in our tribe. It's from the lack of salmon and the introduction of this other food."

"Hostess Twinkies food," I suggest.

"Yeah, exactly. Now diabetes is running crazy in our tribes. We need to restore the fish so our people can live healthy again." To that laudable end not only does he want dredging restricted, he wants hydroelectric dams along the Klamath removed.

The dams. Therein lies yet another factor in the complex ongoing fights being played out in the Jefferson battlegrounds. The farmers want water stored behind the dams to irrigate their crops. They want to continue using the relatively inexpensive electricity generated by the dams' power plants. The tribes and those others who are dependent on salmon need fishery-sustaining cool water flows in the river and access to habitat behind the dams for the spawning salmon. The miners, and the businesses dependent on them, want authority to dredge for gold. The conflicting interests don't talk much and want Sacramento, Salem, and Washington to leave them alone—except when they need services like the firefighting that several days after the lightning struck resulted in the flames snuffed and the Seiad Valley houses spared.

"Scientists, we've got to rethink a lot of things. It's not just one fish, two fish, red fish, blue fish anymore." Ken stops fighting the wind and instead begins packing up his posters and flyers. "We can't just sit here and count the fish until there's zero. With the dam removal people have the chance to be part of one of the biggest restoration projects in history, restoring the Klamath salmon!" He sounds joy filled at the prospect. "You'd think people would want to be involved with that." But as he talks the dream fades. "Not to talk trash, but our Siskiyou County representatives really need to be educated about the whole issue. All of them are pro-farmer as opposed to pro-fish. It is farmer versus fish. Go out to the Scott Valley, they don't like the tribe because we like fish. They talk about being up there for two, three generations, since like the late 1800s. Man! We've been here since the dawn of time. Ten thousand years. We're still here."

"But they're here too."

"We've got to coincide," he reflects. "It's evolution, man. It's not just one big creation and it's all done, evolution after creation. Everybody needs water. Everybody needs to eat fish."

I'm wondering later when I study my notes if he used the wrong word when he said coincide. Did he mean coexist? In fact, he's correct. Coincide may be what they (and we all) need to do. That means occupy the same position simultaneously. Listening to the debate it's all-but-impossible to imagine the settlers and the tribes, the farmers and the fishers, the miners and the environmentalists, the state governments and the Jefferson advocates all coinciding. I'm beginning to see Jefferson as metaphor for the divisiveness paralyzing America.

Chapter Nineteen

A TENTATIVE AGREEMENT

WATER IS TO JEFFERSON WHAT RELIGION IS TO THE MIDDLE EAST. Water is the common denominator that divides the region. Defying generations of Jefferson's history and after years of delicate negotiations, aggressive Jeffersonians vying for each drop of that water negotiated a compromise, and a document titled the Klamath Basin Restoration Agreements was signed in 2010. The deal guaranteed water and cheap power for ranchers and farmers, or compensation if not enough water flowed to them. It gave land back to the Indians and guaranteed adequate water to support the salmon tribes depend on for physical and spiritual nourishment. And it included a radical acknowledgment of error: Four dams along the Klamath were targeted for removal—opening up for salmon long-lost spawning grounds. The coalition of leaders who signed the Agreements represented Indians, environmentalists, farmers and ranchers, fishers and government—both state and local. Interior Secretary Ken Salazar was thrilled, calling it "the largest river restoration project in the world."[57]

California governor Arnold Schwarzenegger traveled to Salem to join his Oregon counterpart and Secretary Salazar for the signing ceremony. Schwarzenegger called the agreement "historic" and an example of "the great things we can achieve by working together." Secretary Salazar continued the theme of the celebratory day: Compromise was replacing conflict. "The Klamath River, which for years was synonymous with controversy, is now a stunning example of how cooperation and partnership can resolve difficult conflicts," crowed Secretary Salazar. "The Agreements provide a path forward to meet the needs of local communities, tribes, farmers, fishermen, and other stakeholders while restoring a beautiful river and its historic salmon runs."[58]

One billion federal dollars would be used to implement the Agreements, money that needed to be allocated by Congress. A final "science-based analysis," as the Interior Department called it, was required by the Agreements, to ensure that destroying the dams would be "in the public interest." That analysis and congressional authorization to spend the billion bucks would seal the deal.

Enter the Klamath County Tea Party Patriots, founded just after the Agreements were signed. Afraid that the deal could deprive Klamath Basin farmers and ranchers of needed irrigation water and cheap electricity, local Tea Party organizers saw the pact as an example of Big Government threatening their independent lifestyle—typical Jeffersonian worries. However government as villain seems an odd characterization for any settler in the Klamath Basin. Big Government is responsible for the vast irrigation network of dams and canals that transformed Jefferson's high desert into a cornucopia of agricultural products. It is Big Government that allowed private enterprise to harvest the timber wealth that built Klamath Falls. It is Big Government that prosecuted the Modoc Wars and marginalized the Indians who were competing with the settlers for the now-fertile land and its bounty. The independent lifestyle heralded by the Klamath County Tea Party Patriots is dependent on Big Government today just as it was yesterday and doubtless will be tomorrow.

But the naysayers were oblivious to that government-citizen interdependence. The Agreements are a deal that "is not going to go anywhere at all," announced rancher and farmer Tom Mallams.[59] He was one of three Klamath County residents so opposed to the Agreements that they were motivated to run for the County Commission and oust pro-Agreement incumbent commissioners.

Chapter Twenty

KLAMATH FALLS DEPRESSION

LAWN SIGNS URGING KLAMATH COUNTY TO VOTE TOM MALLAMS commissioner dot bleak Klamath Falls when I travel to far eastern Jefferson just before the 2012 elections. Before the city limits I can't miss a huge hand-lettered sign informing me that everything President Obama says is a lie. "Bleak," Sheila and I find ourselves repeating to each other as we cruise the struggling downtown.

Murals documenting what used to cover the sides of buildings, like Poole's Pelican Theatre, a showcase for movies that was built in 1929. Farming and ranching built Klamath Falls as a market town, but when the Southern Pacific trains arrived in 1909, the place became a booming high desert city. The railroad connection (documented by another giant mural showing off townsfolk dressed in Sunday best standing in front of locomotive number 2251) meant that the vast timber resources in the Klamath Basin could be exploited. The wood was cut into lumber in Klamath Falls mills, and shipped out to the rest of the world on Southern Pacific trains. The place flourished until the collapse of the Oregon forest products industry, blamed on or credited to the spotted owl—depending on your proclivities.

Main Street is pocked with vacant lots and derelict buildings. Sheila and I cruised it on a Halloween weekend. The sidewalks were packed with children scoring candy from shops and restaurants. Beginning in 2009 the Klamath Falls Downtown Association decided to use Halloween as another opportunity to lure locals back to Main Street. City planning manager Erik Nobel figured about two thousand revelers showed up the weekend we were in town. "It's a chance for the community to come downtown to see the improvements and how wonderful it is," he proclaimed with the civic pride of an ardent booster, quoted in the next day's edition of the *Herald and News*.[60] The newspaper's own downtown building is one of the abandoned ones; the paper relocated across "A" Canal to Foothills Boulevard.

The costumed kiddies paraded around their city's past glory (my favorite was the little boy dressed up as the *Toy Story* cowboy; Sheila's was a little girl toting a basket who was wearing a pioneer outfit with a bonnet that matched her dress and an apron). The stately First National Bank building now houses the El Palacio Mexican restaurant (karaoke!). The Newberry building's show windows are papered over and a sign announces the old five-and-ten-cents store's new incarnation: FUTURE HOME OF DOWNTOWN DOLLAR. But too many of the solid brick buildings languish with empty showroom windows marred by FOR SALE and FOR LEASE and FOR RENT signs. There are other exceptions. One bright spot for us was Murphy's Dogs—a hot dog purveyor. Sheila was looking with disappointment at a sandwich she bought earlier in the day; it lacked onions. I told her tale to Mark, the counterman at Murphy's. He piled a to-go box with both chopped and grilled onions, and he refused to charge for them. "Stop by for a hot dog on your next trip," he said with a typical expression of Oregon Nice. Oregon Nice is pervasive. Throughout Jefferson it's rare to hear a car honk. Strangers hold office and store doors open for each other, and they give up their places in lines for each other. My favorite example of Oregon Nice may be the sign on the paper towel dispenser in the kitchen that serves my office at the University of Oregon. DID YOU USE THE LAST PAPER TOWEL? the note asks, and continues sweetly, PLEASE CONSIDER REFILLING THE DISPENSER. THANK YOU. But there's more: one of those ubiquitous smiley faces.

I compare that with notes in kitchens I've shared in San Francisco offices and back east that yell out things like, YOUR MOTHER DOESN'T WORK HERE. CLEAN UP YOUR OWN MESS, PIGGY!

Downtown's blight is anchored at Main and Esplanade Streets by the surprise of the long-gone Balsiger Ford. The eviscerated building's facade still stands, decorated by the vibrant colors of its Egyptian motif. Bas-relief representations of ancient Egyptian figures wait on either side of the front door for phantom Ford buyers. The dealership was built on the foundation of the gracious five-story White Pelican Hotel, a downtown landmark until it burned in 1926. Around a corner from the Egyptian Revival ruin is another one of the few downtown success stories, Klamath Basin Brewing. The bustling business is housed in the old Crater Lake Creamery building, with the creamery's flashy blue cow neon sign attracting customers to the brewery and its restaurant. But forlorn remnants of another time, like the out-of-business Arcade Hotel, dominate the main drag and nearby streets—punctuated by faded lodgings built for workers

Downtown Klamath Falls has seen better days.

in those days when there was no shortage of good jobs—apartments blocks such as the Hotel Cascade. ALL ROOMS WITH BATH promises the faded painted sign on its red brick wall, the announcement lettered in a typeface popular back when the Pelican Theatre opened.

At the Daily Bagel workers are kept busy making sandwiches named after famous newspapers. I ordered the *New York Times* with no cream cheese. I tore into the sesame-seeded bagel with lox, lettuce, and tomato far north of K-Falls on Highway 97 and found it slathered with mustard and mayonnaise. A couple of doors from the bagel joint the Basin Martini Bar offers UPSCALE CASUAL DINING AND CLASSY COCKTAILS.

The contemporary commercial strips out on Sixth and down Washburn exacerbate the depressed and depressing state of downtown. That's where Jefferson Coin & Watch is located, its sign advertising, BUYING BROKEN AND UNWANTED GOLD JEWELRY. The invasion of Wal-Mart and its ilk were another knockout punch for downtown. This is not only the superficial conclusion by me, a cynical journalist parachuting into Klamath Falls for a couple of days trashing a struggling slice of Jefferson.

My assessment is echoed in the *Herald and News* editorial page. I'm reading the local paper over oatmeal, waiting out the thick, cold fog that's descended over the Basin, adding to the bleakness. "Despite the bad-news-sells theorists," writes *Herald and News* editor Steve Miller, "most local journalists are partial to good news." Miller's is a story boosting local business. But he quotes a friend he identifies only as Joe, a fellow who expresses impressions just like mine of his hometown. "One walk along Main Street," reports Joe, "is enough to curb one's enthusiasm. Vacant storefronts, empty lots and the crumbling Egyptian all speak volumes. More than anything, Klamath Falls suffers from brain drain. Our best and brightest young people just don't stay here. No doubt this area has much to offer. What we need most are jobs. Putting people back to work will cure a lot of ills."[61]

Tom Mallams agrees (who doesn't since unemployment in Klamath County far exceeds national averages) that the county needs jobs. "We need jobs, not empty promises!" he says in his county commissioner campaign literature as he attacks the Klamath Basin Restoration Agreements, and targets what he considers rural Jefferson's ur-villain, the Endangered Species Act (which he refers to repeatedly—as if the voters all would know the abbreviation—as the ESA). "No State in our Nation is immune from the unrelenting wrath of the out of control use of the ESA! This affects more than just timber, agriculture and fishing industries. This economic blight inflicted by the ESA has destroyed countless communities across our Nation. Our industry and private enterprise cannot compete with the rest of the world with our hands tied behind our backs. With the current political climate in place around our Nation, a focused, united attack on the ESA would bring about the necessary reform of the ESA. Never before has our Nation been this willing and prepared to TAKE ON THE ESA! This is indeed a lofty goal, but uniting with our Legislatures can accomplish this."[62] (The exclamation points and capital letters are his.)

When we talk Mallams makes it clear that his distaste for reporters and "the media" about equals his feelings for the Endangered Species Act. He trusts no journalist to report accurately what he calls his "conservative" point of view. The "media" he tells me are not "fair and balanced." Fascinating how that trademarked Fox News phrase is now common currency in the lexicon of those who see journalists as their nemeses. Later, corresponding via e-mail, I reminded Tom Mallams of Thomas Jefferson's opinion. "The press," Jefferson wrote, "is the best instrument for enlightening the mind of man, and improving him as a rational, moral and social being."[63] Mallams also looks to the Founding Fathers for succor, citing them in his campaign harangue about big government. "I believe in private property rights for a reason," he tell us. "Our Founding Fathers, and many others since, demanded and sacrificed for the protection of these rights and I will stand up for preserving the rights of all citizens. You never know when your own individual private property rights may be challenged next. Big government is continually trying to eliminate our rights little by little."[64]

Tom Mallams has harsh words, too, for the University of Oregon, writing it off as a bastion of liberals, particularly expressing disgust for its Environmental Studies Program, which, he tells me, operates in opposition to his own beliefs. A quick look at the Environmental Studies Program mission statement helps put his complaints into perspective: "Our program benefits from the progressive atmosphere and environmental sensitivity of the Eugene community, the cultural heritage of the larger Pacific Northwest, and the natural beauty of the rocky coastline, old-growth forests, and Cascade peaks of western Oregon."[65]

We're enjoying a relatively warm Klamath Falls autumn afternoon. The sun is poking through the Oregon gray. Sheila and I take

What's left of the Klamath Falls namesake.

advantage of the weather to hike along the trail between the Link River and the Keno Canal. We want to take a look at what's left of the city's namesake waterfalls. About a mile up the trail, the irritating sound of trucks on the Highway 97 grade to downtown segues into the tranquil aural massage of Upper Klamath Lake water heading downstream over rock outcroppings toward Karuk tribal lands and on to the Pacific, over 250 miles distant from where we're walking. What was a series of dramatic falls was reduced to today's gentle rapids when hydroelectric dams and irrigation canals built in the early 1900s confined and diverted the Klamath River headwaters. Gigantic stanchions for electricity transmission cables keep us company on our walk, looming over the trail like skeletal Bigfoots, anorexic relatives of the Bigfoot statue keeping watch downriver at the crossroads in Happy Camp. A wedding-dress-white heron is parked in a high tree branch, keeping watch over the Link. We spot a wary mink peeking out behind the rocks that line the banks of the Keno Canal. The trail ends at Upper Klamath Lake, just past the inlet for "A" Canal, the main stream for Klamath Basin irrigation.

Despite its name, there no longer is a waterfall at Klamath Falls.

Chapter Twenty-One

VICE PRESIDENT CHENEY INTRUDES

A DECADE BEFORE TOM MALLAMS AND HIS COLLEAGUES BEGAN their work against the Klamath Basin Restoration Agreements, the Klamath Bucket Brigade came together in the midst of the 2001 severe drought. As Jefferson dried up, federal authorities shut the irrigation sluice gates at Klamath Falls in an effort to keep enough water flowing downriver for endangered fish. The seventh of May is historic for Jefferson. That day in 2001 farmers and ranchers (and their sympathizers from throughout the West) gathered at Veterans Park in Klamath Falls to protest. They carried picket signs adorned with legends like PEOPLE OVER FISH and KLAMATH FARMERS ARE ENDANGERED SPECIES and FEED THE FEDS TO THE FISH.[66] A bucket brigade lined Main Street and beyond. The *Washington Post* estimated it was some ten thousand strong (in a city with a population of only twenty thousand). First the protesters took Upper Klamath Lake water and moved it bucket-by-bucket across town into the original basin irrigation canal, "A" Canal—symbolically violating the law. Next they engaged in direct action: With saws and blowtorches they opened the "A" Canal floodgates sending precious water to parched farms. The Feds repaired the damage. The farms and ranches dried up; crops were ruined.

But the symbolic bucket brigade and the guerilla tactics at the spigot turned into federal government policy the next year when Vice President Dick Cheney engaged the crisis, both because he wanted farmers and ranchers to vote Republican that year in the swing state of Oregon and because, as a Wyoming settler, he sympathized with the water-starved farmers and ranchers. In a *Washington Post* example of important investigative journalism, reporters Jo Becker and Barton Gellma detailed Cheney's troublesome meddling. He used the powers of his office to manipulate and reverse government policies that should be free of politics, tactics telegraphed when President George W. Bush told a Portland crowd in January 2002, "We'll do everything we can to make sure water is available for those who farm."[67] As the *Post* reporters noted, "Law and science seemed to be on the side of the fish. Then the vice president stepped in."[68]

Farmers and ranchers reveled in getting back the water promised them since 1907 when water first flowed from the federal Klamath Project. The Bureau of Reclamation (motto: "Managing Water in the West") dam and diversion project turned more than two hundred thousand arid acres into farm and ranchland. "Let the water flow!" yelped farmers and ranchers in 2002 as Interior Secretary Gale Norton opened a ceremonial floodgate sending water to crops and livestock. Whatever might be left from the settlers' allotment would go downstream for the fish. The result: Later that drought year nearly eighty thousand coho and chinook died in the Klamath, devastating the fishery.

"You can't even begin to imagine what thirty to forty thousand dead fish look like in a twenty-mile radius," reported Yurok Tribal Council chair Susan Masten, after touring the devastated Klamath by boat. "There were fish three, four deep on each side on the banks of the river. There were fish floating down the river. There were hundreds of fish in every eddy. They are starting to smell because they are rotting. I could not have imagined such a horrific scene. It made your heart sicken."[69]

Despite the Cheney Oregon campaigning, Kerry and Edwards beat Bush and Cheney in 2004—in Oregon.

The Klamath Bucket Brigade survives from the 2001-2002 battle of the Jefferson Water Wars as a lobbying organization "adamantly opposed to the Klamath Basin Restoration Agreement." Its motto is "Let Freedom Ring/Let Water Flow" and it posts on its website lengthy articles from a wide variety of sources in an effort to buttress its mission statement, which is to "promote individual and property rights that are vital to the safety, social and economic well-being of the United States."[70]

I browse through the lead article posted on the Bucket Brigade's text-packed website "Mandatory Reading & Knowledge" page. The article is titled "Green Fascism—How Ecological Extremists Seek to Curtail Freedom." The late Edward Zehr is credited for the piece, which was identified as culled from an online publication called the *Washington Weekly*, where it was first published in 2001. Zehr calls environmentalists working on Klamath River issues "eco-nazis" and "greenie-two-shoes mush-heads" promoting what he calls Green Fascism. "Green Fascism envisions depopulation of rural areas and resettlement to urban centers which in time," he wrote, "will come to resemble ant-hills. The environmental movement has been protected from criticism thus far by an intellectually corrupt and morally derelict mainstream press. But the utter vileness of what is happening to the Klamath Basin farmers will eventually work its way into the public's consciousness, despite the best efforts of our 'free' press to spike these stories."[71] The *Washington Weekly* website no longer exists.

It's a quiet afternoon when Sheila and I wander through the all-but empty Klamath County Museum. I find a display case featuring some of the buckets used during the infamous brigade. A plastic pail is marked GRANT COUNTY CHAMBER OF COMMERCE GIVE THE WATER TO THE RANCHERS. A metal one is plastered with a sticker from the Wasco County Public Works Department. Another plastic pail announces in black marker on its side JOSEPHINE COUNTY IS BEHIND YOU! and it's signed by county commissioners. The pail is decorated with a drawing showing the evolution of life forms up a hill from primitive sea creatures to humans—and that human figure is topped by a fish labeled "salmon." A Thomas Jefferson quote is in the case: "The price of freedom is eternal vigilance." It strikes me as odd that there is no explanation for the passing tourist of what the buckets represent. Perhaps the exhibit's curator figures the Bucket Brigade is so well known that the display needs no further details. Or maybe there are few out-of-town visitors to the museum.

When we arrived, the museum staffer who greeted us expressed shock that we hailed from Eugene. "Nobody from Eugene visits Klamath Falls," she told us with certainty. Eugene is infamous in Oregon as a lingering bastion of counterculture. "Nobody moves here," she added.

"Why not?" I asked.

"No jobs," was her simple answer. But in case I missed the obvious evidence she added, "Did you see downtown?"

I checked out some of the other local history noted in the museum. Port Orford may have been the only Jefferson locale bombed by a Japanese aviator during World War II. But on May 5, 1945, just before the war ended, a Japanese balloon bomb killed six Klamath Falls picnickers. This exhibit, which features an example of a balloon-launched bomb, includes an explanation, and calls Klamath County "the only place on the American Continent where death resulted from enemy action during World War II."

In a corner of the museum's exhibit about the brutal Modoc Wars of 1872 and 1873, I spotted a photograph of a grizzled soldier, Brigadier General Jefferson Columbus Davis (*not* the Jefferson Davis who became the president of the Confederacy). After fighting in the war against Mexico and the Civil War, this Jefferson Davis came west and commanded troops against the Klamath tribes until the Modoc Wars ended with the Modoc combatants either exiled from their land, sent to Alcatraz, or hanged.

Chapter Twenty-Two

LIVE FROM THE PEOPLE'S REPUBLIC OF ASHLAND

"ASHLAND IS STUCK IN THE SIXTIES," THE GUIDE AT THE KLAMATH County Museum told me about her Jefferson neighbors when we were talking about the sad state of Klamath Falls. Ashland is sixty miles and a world away from Klamath Falls, but it's hardly stuck in the sixties.

State Route 66 (no connection with the more famous "get your kicks on Route 66") winds its two lanes over the spectacular Cascades through towering firs (and the stumps of their logged cousins) and past verdant meadowlands. This is the territory of the Cascade-Siskiyou National Monument and the route of the Applegate branch of the Oregon Trail—blazed by Jesse Applegate in 1846 when the American pioneers heading west sought a route south of British forts along the Columbia River.[72] That same year the Brits and Yanks agreed that the 49th parallel would divide their Northwest claims, the Americans securing what they called Oregon Country and the British the Columbia District.

We stop for a look at the John C. Boyle Dam, one of the Klamath dams targeted for removal by the Agreements. Built in the 1950s, the dam—just a few miles west of Klamath Falls—juxtaposes its concrete-and-steel industrial hulk of walls and pipes and girders on the bucolic Jefferson countryside. It backs the river up into the lake-like, wide and placid John C. Boyle Reservoir, which stores water to drive the turbines of the John C. Boyle Powerhouse. John C. Boyle was a Jeffersonian. Born in Ft. Jones on the California side, he studied engineering at Stanford, graduated in 1910, and returned north to mastermind projects that generated electricity on the Umpqua, Rogue, and Klamath Rivers.[73] His legacy remained heroic for years: he tamed the rivers and provided cheap power. Such massive works were created during that era by men remarkably unconcerned with the conflicting interests the Agreements negotiators struggled with a couple of generations later. I watch as a man throws a ball for his dog, the dog runs fast to chase it, and jumps into the cold John C. Boyle Reservoir water after it. It's a lovely scene—just a man and his dog out in what looks like the wild—a sight free at first superficial glance from harsh conflicts dividing Jeffersonians.

PacificCorps, the power company that owns and operates the dam and the hydroelectric generator just downstream from it, agreed to its destruction as a dollars-and-cents business proposition. Accountants for PacificCorps determined that keeping the aging facility humming and licensed would cost more money than the complex makes for the company.

Tom Mallams, whose ranch benefits from the still-cheap electricity generated by the PacificCorps Klamath dams, heartily disagrees with what he sees as corporate capitulation to environmentalists and the tribes. "Those dams provide very cheap, cheap, cheap power," he exudes. "I mean, it's the cheapest power generation there possibly is."

Of course cost depends on what one values. Jeff Mitchell is a Klamath tribal councilman and with the dams removed he envisions a free-flowing Klamath teeming with resurgent fish life. "When the creator put us here he also provided us with a resource that sustained us for thousands of years," is Mitchell's point of view. "I literally wouldn't be here if it wasn't for those fish. My people wouldn't be here. So we feel it's a responsibility of ours to make sure that those fish survive."[74]

A valiant attempt at transcending polarized Jefferson politics.

At the Pinehurst Inn, a Highway 66 roadhouse since the 1920s, I find an attempt at temporary and alcohol-fueled reconciliation. The signboard out front beckons weary travelers not just with chicken pot pie and prime rib but also from 5 p.m. to 7 p.m. a BIPARTISAN HAPPY HOUR! with NO POLITICAL DISCUSSIONS ALLOWED.

The panorama opens up to a vast view of the Rogue Valley down past emigrant Lake to Ashland, a city I know well. Back in the early 1970s, my parents moved from Sausalito, lured north by the enticing bubble that is Ashland: a cosmopolitan community just across the California line, nestled at the base of Mt. Ashland and looking out across the Rogue Valley. With its world-renowned Shakespeare plays, the sprawling city park along Lithia Creek, and Southern Oregon University, Ashland is a tourist destination city with a healthy economy, especially when compared with its struggling neighbors a few miles north like Medford and Grants Pass, or east back over 66, such as Klamath Falls.

Ashland feels more like north-northern California than Oregon. The climate is warmer and dryer than Grants Pass, which is less than an hour up I-5. The hills in late summer glow golden from the dried grasslands. California-style craggy oak trees spot those hills. The shops and restaurants, and the bed-and-breakfast inns look like what Port Orford's mayor fantasizes about for his forlorn stretch of Oregon coastline. Ashland's trendy women's clothing stores and its eateries stocked with organic this and gluten-free that, its swank downtown Lithia Springs hotel, its revitalized 1950s-era motels (the neon sign at the Palm glows retro hip) and its well-stocked bookstore named Bloomsbury, all are competitive with California dreams like Carmel-by-the-Sea. Ashland these days feels as if it came alive from the advertising pages of *the New Yorker*, *Travel + Leisure,* and *Vogue*.

Wander through Lithia Park. Stop in the plaza downtown and drink the foul-tasting Lithia water from Lithia Springs (it's supposedly curative). Sip an organic beer at the Standing Stone Organic Brewery. Take in a play performed on the Shakespeare Festival's Elizabethan stage. Linger over a sidewalk dinner and then dance until late. Ashland exhibits a sophisticated European-style elegance not found elsewhere in Jefferson. This combination of the urbane with small-town Americana (soda fountains!) is what attracted my parents to Ashland at a time when some Oregonians were circling their wagons, or at least the memories of the wagons their antecedents used to cross the continent on the Oregon Trail when *they* invaded the territory.

DON'T CALIFORNICATE OREGON! was a familiar bumper sticker and billboard of that era. Conservationist Tom McCall was governor and famously told a national television interviewer, "Come visit us again and again. But for heaven's sake, don't come here to live."[75] Nonetheless the Californians came north, their wallets bulging with real estate equity. Ashland prospered. Port Orford is where Jefferson was founded, and Yreka is its political capital. The farms and ranches of the Klamath River Basin and Klamath Falls breed its revolutionaries (and reactionaries). And Ashland is its cultural crossroads.

On the Southern Oregon University campus, I make my way into the basement offices of Jefferson Public Radio. On the wall hangs a photograph of Judge John Childs, identified without caveat as Jefferson's first governor. I take a seat in the studio across from the host of *The Jefferson Exchange*, the network's daily talk show.

"Coming up after the news, the state of mind that is the State of Jefferson," announces Geoffrey Riley. "The far ends of California and Oregon did once consider splitting off and forming a separate state, but it never happened. For one thing, the attack on Pearl Harbor changed the national focus instantly." With that he kicked off an hour of us talking Jefferson with Jeffersonians. "State of mind or state of possibilities?" he asked.

Before we start our chat, Riley catches his audience up on the status of the fires burning throughout Jefferson Public Radio's listening area. Residents of Seiad Valley have been told to prepare to evacuate. That fire is spreading fast through the mountains where I saw it burning from the firehouse during the volunteer fire department fundraiser. The terrain is so steep on the north side of the river that firefighters were unable to use bulldozers as they attempted to clear a firebreak.

"Now it's more of an idea," Riley says about Jefferson, dismissing potential statehood. He asked me what intrigues me about Jefferson and it made me rethink my fascination with this phenomenon I've been researching. Much of my academic and journalism work deals with borders, migration, and identity. I see in Jefferson the same sorts of issues and conflicts that plague other border regions I study, from the Mexico line that marks where California and the rest of the

States start, to Eastern Europe and the residue of the days when the Iron Curtain cut it off from its cousins to the west. Do Jeffersonians really want to play the role of Yugoslavians and break away from Oregon and California? Could an entity as small and as poor as Jefferson would be, were it free of Salem and Sacramento, sustain itself? How is it that the natives and the settlers still cannot seem to find peaceful coexistence? Why can't the farmers and ranchers figure out a water sharing agreement that keeps alive a vibrant fishery for those seeking salmon in the rivers and in the Pacific? How is it that environmental activists and descendants of the original non-native settlers can't find common ground when they both claim a spiritual affinity for the wilderness? These are issues, I've come to conclude, that are metaphors for the divisiveness that continues to split the nation into red and blue camps. Politically, socially, and culturally, contemporary America is as far apart as trailer park owner Bruce Johnson and Karuk biologist Ken Brink. There are lessons of value to be learned from Jefferson for our national political paralysis, for the coarse civic dialogues and gross disagreements regarding cultural and political norms. Growing distrust of government, confusion over what constitutes a vibrant democracy, the rise of populist leaders—all dissonant factors on the national stage—read as relentless chapters in the regional story of Jefferson. The disenfranchisement those who self-identify as Jeffersonians feel serves as a reference point for better understanding of the crises facing government throughout America. Maybe Jefferson is the petri dish example of a devolving American dream.

The radio network tells its listeners that it is broadcasting to the mythical State of Jefferson, but when Sheriff Dean Wilson announces that he will not enforce laws passed in Sacramento and Washington with which he disagrees, Jefferson no longer is just a myth. The image of a gun-toting cowboy sauntering down the street in Crescent City with an illegal six-gun on his hip who waves a "howdy" to an unconcerned sheriff gives Jefferson a reality that does not rely on the official complications of secession. The sheriff proves that Jeffersonians can separate themselves from California and Salem regarding some of their complaints without the bother of a formal disengagement. Just do what you want far from the urban powers and dare the state authorities to come and stop you.

"You're as far as you can get from Salem and Sacramento and still be within the state," Riley says about Jefferson. He believes that the distance from seats of power adds to a sense of alienation—it's not just philosophical disagreements, it's mileage. No question he's correct, but there is an equal amount of alienation between the disparate groups that inhabit the remote mountains and valleys of Jefferson. This kind of us-against-them mentality in tiny communities where most people know each other intimately is reminiscent of the relationships and conflicts that led to the violent breakup of Yugoslavia. The rhetoric is intense, personal, and without compromise.

"When you talk about the mythical State of Jefferson it sounds so heartwarming," I tell Riley about his network's identification of its place, "but on the ground the infighting is more than discomforting—it's dangerous."

The phone rings and Riley welcomes a listener named Skeeter to his program.

"Are you familiar with a book called *Ecotopia* by Ernest Callenbach, written in the mid 1970s?" Skeeter asks.

Of course. *Ecotopia* is that novel set in a future (for the 1970s) Pacific Northwest that secedes from the United States to form a more ecologically sound society than the smog-spewing United States.

"The reason that I ask," continues Skeeter, "is that I am curious if you have heard any rumblings of creating something like that. In my mind it seems like we could have an economic secession where we would have a dual currency. Federal dollars for those who would want to use that and a separate currency that is accepted on the local or regional level." Skeeter's attitude is so Jeffersonian: Let's do it for ourselves, let's keep it local. In fact, anti–National Monument activist Anthony Intiso has a stash of silver Jefferson coins—Double X silver dollars—that were minted as collectors' items and sold out quickly, with a hefty numismatic value added to their face value price of the silver. I tried to convince him to sell just one to me, but he's keeping them all for himself. Skeeter, with a nod to *Ecotopia*, wants to see a Jefferson that keeps its tax money at home. The problem with that strategy was made clear by the California legislative analyst back in 1941 who did the math and pointed out that Sacramento sent more value in cash and services to Jefferson than Jefferson sent in taxes to the capital. More recently I spoke with one of Jefferson's historians, the late James Rock, author of the book *State of Jefferson: The Dream Lives On*.

"Is it a dream or a nightmare to create a new state out of an impoverished region?" I asked Rock, who agreed that the numbers don't look good.

"The nightmare part of it would be that there is no economic base to support a state in southern Oregon and northern California," said the longtime Yreka resident. "We cost Oregon and California more to support I-5 than we contribute from these counties. If you would form a state, you'd have another Appalachia because there simply is no base to support it."

"Leave us alone or give us more?" talk show host Geoffrey Riley wonders over the air about what Jeffersonians would prefer regarding their relationship with Salem and Sacramento. No question in my mind that most of the Jeffersonians I've been meeting would answer, "Leave us alone," at least until they found themselves forced to try and replicate what the two states provide in services. Jeffersonian separatists don't want a state government dominated by Portland, San Francisco, and Los Angeles telling them what to do, a government controlled by urban dwellers who, they are convinced, don't know or care what life is like up in sparsely populated Jefferson.

Riley read an e-mail from a listener named Scott who identified himself as someone who grew up in the Rogue Valley. He questioned if Oregonians would really like to join with Californians to create a separate state. "I never heard anyone here seriously advocate joining forces with California," he wrote. "Emotional affinities on this side of the border have always been strongly Oregonian in my experience. The idea of combining some of the most economically depressed counties of Oregon with some of the most economically depressed counties of California and subjecting ourselves to government out of Redding wouldn't sound appealing to many people in Jackson County." Scott raises a sobering aspect of devolving government toward more and more local control. What is local enough to satisfy those who are frustrated with what they consider is government out of touch with their needs and desires? Scott called the State of Jefferson "just a benign fairy tale."

The hour on the radio passed quickly, but not before Riley and I mused about the origin of the Jefferson name. Was it picked to honor the third president of the United States, Thomas Jefferson, because he authored the Declaration of Independence, and because he sent Lewis & Clark on the expedition that explored the Pacific Northwest and accelerated the migration of pioneers to Jefferson? Or was it named after Jefferson Davis, the president of the Confederacy, to honor the heritage of settlers who fought for the South and chose to move to the Pacific Northwest rather than remain in their defeated homeland after the Civil War? Or could it have been named after Jefferson C. Davis, the general who defeated the natives in the Modoc Wars (and presided over the hanging of four captured Indians)?

For those who might consider it unlikely that Oregonians would name a place after a celebrated personage's first name, consider my new hometown, Eugene. The city is named after its founder, Eugene Franklin Skinner. The official naming is marked as January 8, 1850, when the post office chose to identify the Willamette Valley crossroads as Eugene. Local boosters were eager to jettison the common name for trading post: The future home of the University of Oregon Ducks was referred to until the post office opened as Skinner's Mudhole.

General Jefferson C. Davis did not party to authority he disliked. During the Civil War he shot and killed his superior officer, General William Nelson, after the two argued in the Galt House hotel in Louisville. Nelson slapped Davis in the face and called him a coward. "This is not the last of it," Davis announced. He borrowed a pistol from another soldier in the lobby, returned to Nelson, and shot him dead. General Davis was never charged with the crime and returned to active Civil War duty.[76] He soldiered on until his death.[77]

Oregon's history suggests either of the two statesmen (or even the general) is a possibility as the source of the 51st state's name. Before the territory became a state, the Oregon Provisional Government declared it illegal in 1848 for a "Negro" or a "Mulatto" to reside in the Oregon Territory. When Oregon was admitted to the Union in 1859, that exclusion was included in the state's constitution. The clause in question makes sobering reading: "No free Negro, or Mulatto, not residing in this state at the time of the adoption of this constitution, shall come, reside, or be within this state, or hold any real estate, or make any contracts, or maintain any suit therein; and the Legislative Assembly shall provide by penal laws, for the removal, by public officers, of all such Negroes, and Mulattos, and for their effectual exclusion from the state, and for the punishment of persons who shall bring them into the state, or employ, or harbor them." Perhaps even more sobering is the fact that the clause was not removed until 1926. The Ku Klux Klan was active throughout Jefferson in the 1920s. There is a long history of prejudice against the Other in Oregon.

Indeed, the oft-quoted Jefferson Davis 1861 inauguration address plea, "All we ask is to be left alone," would work well as a state motto for many of the Jeffersonians I encountered during my research treks around the mythical state.

Chapter Twenty-Three

THE JEFFERSON RESURGENCE

A COUPLE OF WEEKS AFTER MY VISIT TO SEIAD VALLEY AND HAPPY Camp I'm back on I-5 speeding south from Ashland toward Yreka. I clear the California border at the bug station with my usual "No" to the "Do you have any fruits or vegetables?" question. The crossing is as easy as accepting a "Proclamation of Independence" at a Jefferson roadblock in 1941. On this trip Mt. Shasta looms into sight with its usual dominating presence, some late summer snow patches sparkling near the peak. The fire that was threatening Seiad Valley homes and Rick Jones's store—and which burned on both sides of the state line—is, Jefferson Pubic Radio tells me, contained.

I pull off of the freeway at Yreka, such a much more vibrant city than its vanquished rival for the capital of Jefferson, Port Orford. Once Mayor Gable died, no charismatic replacement personality from the coast joined the Jefferson movement. The lasting symbol of Jefferson in something akin to open rebellion became the well-publicized roadblocks on Highway 99. Since 1941, Yreka—at least for the outside world—is hometown for the Jefferson myth.

The main street—Miner Street—is lined with solid and handsome red brick buildings from the Gold Rush days, testimonials to the wealth that the gold around Yreka created. Miner Street bustles still. The Palace Barber Shop operates two chairs. Cooley

& Pollard Hardware is displaying lawn mowers and rototillers on the sidewalk in front of the store. Across the street, a notice on the D.D. Colton Building recognizes David Colton, a writer who found better diggings in journalism than for gold when he founded the *Mountain News Herald*. The neon sign is lit at Ohlund's Office Supply. An American flag flies out in front of Ming's Chinese restaurant.

At the Yreka Chamber of Commerce storefront a banner in the show window bellows, WELCOME TO YREKA CAPITAL OF THE STATE OF JEFFERSON SINCE 1941. On the sidewalk a rusting mine cart overflows with petunias and Sweet Williams. At the court-house where John C. Childs announced he was assuming the governorship, a sculpture of Jefferson-backer and longtime state senator from the region Randolph Collier sits. He looks dapper from head to toe in bowtie and wingtips. "The Father of the Free-ways," as the adjacent plaque anoints him, shares a park bench with a relaxed-looking man.

Jefferson banner in a Yreka store window.

"Having a conversation with Randy?" another fellow says as he walks up to join his friend, who acts as if it's a line he's heard before.

The two walk off, leaving me alone with Randy. Senator Collier was a Siskiyou County native son, born in Etna and first elected to the California legislature in 1938. Not so long after the 1941 Jefferson advocates packed up their long guns, pistols, and road-blocks, Senator Collier coauthored the Collier-Burns Highway Act of 1947, which led to the spaghetti of Autobahns connecting Californians. Ironic, considering his alliance with the road-seeking Jeffersonians: Most of the freeways Senator Collier helped create were built far from Jefferson down in southern California. Other than its I-5 backbone, Jefferson is spared the freeway culture of off ramps littered with fast-food joints. Those 1941 theatrics in Yreka that Senator Collier helped orchestrate led to the periodic and con-tinuing efforts to create some sort of State of Jefferson—promoted by entrepreneurs and regionalists, along with politicians both ama-teur and professional.

The year 1971 was a resurgent one for Jefferson. On the Ore-gon side, Josephine County Commissioner Kenneth W. Jackson traveled to a meeting of Oregon counties far across the state in Pendleton, carrying with him Jefferson T-shirts and a double cross flag. He promoted what would be—now that Alaska and Hawaii were part of the Union—the 51st state, advertising Grants Pass (his county seat) as its capital. Down in California at the same time, Siskiyou County Supervisor Earl Ager was remembering his days back in 1941, parading for Jefferson on the streets of Yreka. He agreed that the cause was still valid, but wanted the capital on the California side of the line.[78] Supervisor Ager spouted radical goals for a Jefferson he proposed to lead as its first governor, and he insisted that—unlike the heritage of the 1941 action—his call for Jefferson was no "publicity stunt." Vigilantes instead of police would be the answer to street criminals, he bragged. "The people of northern California and southern Oregon would take care of these sons of bitches. They wouldn't need police." This elected county official had ideas for those already tried and convicted of crimes. "There's a lotta guys in prison that oughta be hung. If they hung 'em the first time they were put in prison they wouldn't have to worry about putting them there a second time."

Supervisor Ager's target was not just the criminal justice system. He wanted to protect Jefferson's natural resources from exploitation by southern California and northern Oregon. "I think we could pull our own weight in Jefferson just fine," he told Redding newspaper reporter Garth Sanders Jr. in November 1971, thirty years after "Governor" Childs in his inauguration address claimed such independence. "All we'd have to do is shut the water off to southern California and we'd have no problem bargaining with them." Reporter Sanders helps us get a sense of Earl Ager's personality. In his front page story with its banner headline, Sanders tells us Supervisor Ager "snorted" and "snapped" his answers to questions, including the crucial, "Who should be the governor of Jefferson?"

"Me, that's who!" he snorted and snapped.[79]

In 1978 a depressed Klamath Falls turned to the Jefferson legend for help and staged the Jefferson State Stampede rodeo. The Oregon governor at the time, Vic Atiyeh, rode in the Main Street parade and joined Klamath Falls lawyer and longtime state legislator Harry Boivin for what the two called a summit meeting. Boivin was anointed governor of Jefferson for the duration of the rodeo. Klamath Falls funeral home director Jim Ward served as Jefferson secretary of state during the rodeo days. "It was just to try to get some business stirred up," he said later. "The downtown area was slumping, and things were at a dead end here."[80]

The *San Francisco Chronicle* sent reporter Kevin Fagan up to Jefferson in 2008 to check on the status of the story the paper created back in 1941. Reporter Fagan found Randy Bashaw, a Trinity County lumber mill manager, complaining in the crossroads of Hayfork. "We have nothing in common with you people down south. Nothing," insisted Bashaw. "The sooner we're done with all you people, the better."

In Yreka he found another complaining voice at Cooley & Pollard Hardware where manager Richard Mitchell told him about Jefferson, "Heck, yeah, it's a darn good idea. Those liberal people down south don't understand us at all."[81]

Chapter Twenty-Four

Journalist Turned Activist

I abandon I-5 at Yreka and tour westward on State Route 3 into the Scott Valley. Hay barns are stacked high with golden bales. Irrigation apparatus showers fields with water while adjacent dry land sits fallow, decorated with flowering sagebrush. Stands of towering pine line the two-lane blacktop as I approach Etna. Storybook farmhouses dot the picturesque landscape. I pull into the gravel parking lot at Bob's Ranch House Restaurant, get out of the Volvo, and stretch my legs before going inside to find a quiet table.

"I'd like some juice," I request of the waitress when she comes by and asks me if I want something to drink.

"Do I get to pick?" is her smart waitress-talk response, and I interpret it to mean she intends to tolerate outsider me, busy piling my notebook and camera on the table. Etna's official population is 737. That means she knows who's local and who's not. Plus my white linen slacks and dark blue dress shirt undoubtedly look too citified for this isolated farming valley. But I immediately feel at home at Bob's Ranch House. The waitress's "Do I get to pick?" is a phrase from a universal all-American restaurant lexicon that I translate to a guarded variation of "Welcome." Just how welcome is going to be balanced by my banter back—whether I know the language.

"Depends on what you've got," I say, and her half smile along with the litany, "Orange, tomato, cranberry, and apple," mean I pass the initial test.

Journalist Liz Bowen rouses the rabble.

Along with my apple juice, Liz Bowen joins me at the table. I've come to Etna to meet the founder of Pie N Politics, a website Bowen created in 2010 to counter what she and others consider false propaganda often generated by government agencies, environmental activists ("Greenies" to use Bowen's terminology), and the Karuk tribe.

"Citizens in Siskiyou County are finding government regulations are destroying their RIGHTS," Liz Bowen announces on Pie N Politics to explain her point of view. "This includes Water Rights, Property Rights and Individual Rights [the capital letters are hers]. We believe in the Constitutions of the United States and the State of California that provide RIGHTS for its citizens. We also believe these RIGHTS are being systematically reduced, which is resulting in tyranny from our governments—at all levels. Under the U.S. Constitution, the government should serve the people!"

Daughter of ranchers with deep roots in Scott Valley and wife of a former rancher ("It's just too hard to make a living," she says about her family's exit from that life), Bowen worked as a journalist for years, covering agriculture issues for the now-defunct local weekly *Pioneer Press*. Her father arrived in Scott Valley in 1928 from Arizona "just before the Depression," she notes, during which he and his brothers lost their ranches. They survived, she tells me, by working as hands on ranches repossessed by banks. It's a heritage that informs the politics she preaches: The property rights of individual Americans are in jeopardy. "Over regulation hurts the local economy," she says, citing what she calls the demise of the Jefferson timber industry as a prime example.

Liz Bowen says she started Pie N Politics to network with others concerned about local Scott Valley politics. Quickly the website evolved to embrace the strident international politics of the Tea Party. "I'm putting forth the truth that I know, the truth that I've lived. The science," she says about studies cited by "greenies," the Karuks, and government agencies, "gets so frustrating to me because the science seems to get twisted. It just feels like people keep taking our stuff."

A few days after we spoke I checked her latest Pie N Politics postings. WILD BILL IS RIGHT, reads a headline, with a subhead that states, "Claiming racism does make money for Obama." The Wild Bill referred to by Bowen is a fellow with another website (Wild Bill for America) who files strident commentaries on YouTube while wearing western clothing and talking tough. He calls himself "Our God and Country Commentator." In the rant cited by Bowen, Wild Bill (no last name and no contact information is available on his site) condemns a class action suit on behalf of black farmers and—with no documentation—charges then-Senator Obama with "fraud against the American people."

Bowen wrote a dispatch on Pie N Politics with a Crescent City dateline, a report on a Support Rural American Sheriffs (an organization that bolsters so-called constitutional sheriffs) rally that was held in the Del Norte County seat (where Dean Wilson wears the sheriff's star). "Some bureaucrats in high levels of a few state and federal agencies are regulating activities that greatly affect life and livelihoods in rural areas," she wrote. "Citizens facing over-regulation feel attacked from newly-designated agency permits for legal irrigation water, timber harvesting or fishing rights. Escalating fees and gigantic fines are attached to the newly written codes and regulations. Sheriff Wilson," her dispatch continued, "believes there is 'hope' in standing on the Constitution as the 'law of the land.' Additionally, the Bill of Rights protects liberties and freedoms for the individual. It is under the U.S. Constitution where local governments are provided equal rights. So these men [sheriffs such as Dean Wilson] are speaking, standing up and claiming their equality to the chagrin of a few government employees, socialists, and leftists."

Featured on Pie N Politics is a poem by Siskiyou County rancher Roy Smith, which starts: "We have to save the coho salmon/But the records are so very new/Was there ever very many/Was there always just a few?/They ruined families, homes and towns/So the spotted owl could have its way./But we've never really heard/If the owl is better off today."

"There's enough water for both ranchers and fish if you understand how nature works," Bowen says, dismissing Karuk biologist Ken Brink's concern about coho, her blonde hair complemented by her bright blue blouse and eyes. She points to what she says is the fish-healthy Shasta River, packed with hearty returning chinook salmon and void of many coho. Maybe the chinook eat the coho, she offers, quoting from an unnamed study, or maybe the coho simply don't like that river. "When the snow melt is gone," she says, "there's not enough water for fish or ranchers. The water is gone, and the ranchers learn to live with that." So must the fish, she says, because using water is a

private property right of the ranchers and farmers living for generations in Scott Valley.

"Come walk a mile in our shoes before you start telling us how
to do things," is her message to the environmental activists who seek
more water in wilder rivers for a healthier fishery. "We're not the
stupid country bumpkins that a lot of people claim we are." She calls
ranchers and farmers food producers, more concerned about the
health of their land and their animals than political organizing. "My
husband worked on a ranch out here where typically, by the end of
June, there was no more surface irrigation water from Etna Creek."
Water rights to a majority of the water from the creek were controlled by another ranch. "We didn't whine and complain about it.
That's the way it is. Our water is gone the middle of June. You figure
what kind of crop you can raise. You put your cattle on it in April and
May and June. As soon as there's no more water, you move the cattle
off before you've ruined the pasture. We do know how to take care
of the land. We're feeling very much like we're constantly attacked,
that everything we do is wrong." She repeats her invitation. "Come
and walk a mile in our shoes and maybe you'll understand why we
do the things we do."

I can appreciate her frustration with the criticism. Ranchers and
farmers have been pulling water out of Etna Creek for generations.
But times have changed. We've learned about causes and effects we
didn't know about when we started irrigating the arid valley. Perhaps the fishery is suffering because diverted water is ruining their
habitat. Maybe the lifestyles of Scott Valley settlers should adapt to
preserve the fish.

"Is there any validity to an argument that this land should no
longer be ranched and farmed?" I ask.

Her answer comes without hesitation. "Not if you believe in the
Constitution of the United States. We have a right to live and work
where we would like to live and work." Besides, she says, it's not

practical to turn enormous swaths of Jefferson into wildlife refuges. "The trees are overgrown," she says about those places where logging is prohibited, "and we're seeing huge wildfires that are devastating to wildlife. Nature is not always beautiful and perfect. Nature is very chaotic."

"Is there any validity to an argument that this is not an ideal place for ranching?" I take the devil's advocate position with Liz Bowen. After all, her family has experienced tough times trying to make a living from the often-unforgiving land. I offer a stretch along the Willamette River in downtown Portland as an example. The freeway was razed after locals realized it was inefficient, ugly, and ruined access to the riverfront. A broad park that serves as the city's gracious backyard replaced the noisy eyesore.

She rejects the premise. "No, it's a beautiful area for ranching. You yourself said it was beautiful." I did indeed, because it is. "The reason it's beautiful is because that land is pasture—alfalfa. That's water that's creating it. It's green and beautiful here because of the livelihood. You supposedly go natural, it might be beautiful to someone, but it will be very different. It won't have the green."

"It won't have you and your neighbors," I point out. "You'll move."

She agrees. "We just feel like we're constantly being attacked," she complains about the "greenies" working with the Karuk tribe and environmental organizations such as Klamath-Siskiyou Wild in Ashland. "We feel like we are very good stewards of the land, and we feel like their goal is to remove us. If we can't make a livelihood here, they will have done their job."

"What would their motivation be to want to remove you from the land?" I ask.

"Do you want me to get into Agenda 21?" she asks back. "If you control the water, you control the people. If you destroy the idea that people can own property and make a living on that property, then you're controlling the people."

Chapter Twenty-Five

JEFFERSON, THE UNITED NATIONS, AND THE POWER OF TALK SHOWS

AGENDA 21 IS THE BOOGEYMAN THAT REPRESENTS—FOR THOSE who fear it—the ultimate conspiracy by the United Nations and its enablers to deny Americans like Liz Bowen their God-given and constitutional rights. It is a detailed document (available in its original and complete text via a quick Internet search) outlining a model for addressing a myriad of global crises: poverty, overpopulation, human health, sustainable development, and the environment. Its preamble suggests the world might do well working together to solve these border-crossing challenges. "No nation can achieve this on its own," Agenda 21 states about dealing with hunger, ill health, illiteracy, and the deterioration of ecosystems, "but together we can—in a global partnership for sustainable development."[82]

"Go look this one up, because it's not so harmless," fearmonger Glenn Beck advised viewers of his Fox News talk show about Agenda 21 (the episode is available as a link on the Pie N Politics website). He waves the thick document at the camera and, as he pulls out a page at the top of the report, tells his audience with a smirk, "It doesn't get spooky until about here." Then he reads this line as the text is displayed on the screen: "Developed countries and funding agencies should provide specific assistance to developing countries in adopting an enabling approach for the provision of shelter for all." At this point in the commentary Beck smirks at the camera again

and interprets the fragment for those watching, "So that's like guaranteed housing! Well that's going to be great 'cause the government is
going to own all of our houses anyway because we're all going broke!"
He laughs, and then feigns a serious look as he summarizes, "Reading though the pages," he flips through it for the camera as he talks,
"it's clear that 'sustainable development' is just a nice way of saying
'centralized control over all of human life on planet earth.'" He puts
down the document and adds a condescending, "That doesn't sound
bad." Before the Fox News episode concludes, Beck adds George
Soros to his rogues' gallery of globalists seeking (and bankrolling)
"centralized control over all human life."

Glenn Beck isn't the only critic of Agenda 21; he just may be
its most entertaining one (for those amused by his act). In Jefferson, count Liz Bowen as one of those critics. "Yes," she wrote in an
e-mail message to me when I queried her about Soros and Agenda
21, "there is a direct line from George Soros to several 'projects' in
the State of Jefferson area."

There is a need for a separate Jefferson state, Bowen told me,
because of the region's locale far from seats of California and Oregon
government and the nearest big cities, San Francisco and Portland.
"I truly believe in the Constitution, and that local control is the best
for each community. Leaders need to be local enough that they can
hear and feel what the local people want. That doesn't mean we all
get what we want," she adds with a note of *realpolitik*.

"But there will never be a State of Jefferson," I forecast.

She laughs a dismissive laugh. "You never know what happens
in the future. In the history of mankind, there's constantly change,
constantly evolution, attrition."

No argument from me, and I tell her stories about living in Berlin
just before the Berlin Wall was breached and Germany was unified.
No one—not politicians, families asunder since the Wall was built, or
we journalists covering the Cold War—predicted its demise in our

lifetimes. Except perhaps Ronald Reagan when he called across it in 1987, "Mr. Gorbachev, tear down this wall!"

"We've seen whole civilizations go by the wayside," Bowen says. "We are fighting for how we want to live. We believe there should be a separate state to support this area. People in San Francisco have to walk more than a mile in our shoes to understand. We don't go to San Francisco or Portland and tell them how they should be running their area. We would like to be able to govern ourselves. We in the State of Jefferson believe in the Constitution. We believe in local control." Even as she insists she is not opposed to the state and federal governments, she says, "We believe we, as a community, can take better care of ourselves."

We shake hands and Liz Bowen leaves the Ranch House Restaurant while I puzzle over her terminology. "We in the State of Jefferson believe in the Constitution." I keep the US Constitution on my desk (the pocket-sized copy courtesy of the American Civil Liberties Union). But I find it odd to believe *in* the Constitution. It is a document that outlines the basic structures of our government, and as a journalist I'm particularly enamored of its First Amendment. We believe in God or we believe in the tooth fairy because we cannot produce God or the tooth fairy at our command. The Constitution exists; there's no need to believe in it. You can respect it, embrace it, amend it, or even violate it. And you can study its origin. It was during the 1787 Constitutional Convention that the document was drafted and it wasn't until 1790 that Rhode Island ratified it, finally bringing all thirteen colonies into the Union. In only three colonies was the vote to adopt the Constitution unanimous. Many patriots in Virginia, then the largest state both in land mass and number of people, balked at the strong federal government agreed to by the delegates who drafted the Constitution.

Patrick Henry (he of "Give me liberty or give me death!" Revolutionary War fame) railed against the proposed Constitution when it was debated at the state's ratifying convention in 1788. "This Constitution is said to have beautiful features," he lectured his colleagues, "but when I come to examine these features they appear to me horribly frightful. Among other deformities, it has an awful squinting; it squints toward monarchy; and does not this raise indignation in the breast of every true American? Your President may easily become king." He wasn't alone. The Virginia vote was a close 89 to 79 to accept the Constitution, with Patrick Henry and other opponents throughout the former colonies worrying that it jeopardized the very liberty and local control Liz Bowen now sees it championing.

"I see the need for the State of Jefferson because we are far away from the capitals," Bowen says. "Local control is the best for each community, city and region. We would like to govern ourselves."

Chapter Twenty-Six

DEPOPULATED WILDERNESS
AND URBAN ZOOS

IT WAS AT QUIGLEY'S STORE IN KLAMATH RIVER WHERE I STOPPED to ask about the NO MONUMENT signs I was seeing spotted along Highway 96. There cordial Ann Hansen told me that one Anthony Intiso could explain the controversy from the No Monument point of view and she rummaged around behind the counter finally producing a piece of paper for me with his telephone number noted on it. "We're

On the Klamath River Highway.

free here," Hansen told me about her life in the tiny riverside community when I asked her about the No Monument campaign, "and Congress wants to control us. They want to charge a toll," she said about the highway, "and tell us what we need to do and knock off the freedom here. We take care of each other." When I pressed her for particulars about "knocking off the freedom" and "charging a toll," she pleaded ignorance and suggested I call the number she offered.

Those casting for characters for a western movie may wish to check in with the charismatic Anthony Intiso, the charming fellow who answered the phone at the number Hansen provided. He's quick to smile and laugh, and he sports a Dali-esque moustache with handlebars that point up toward his bald pate. He could play the county sheriff. In fact his career as a polymath is so varied, I would not have been surprised had he added sheriff to his long list of professions. He earned a law degree, bowled professionally, worked for the government as chief of the Ventura County road department, and was an entrepreneur who bought and sold businesses throughout the West. On the side he owned and operated a gold mine in the Los Padres National Forest between Los Angeles and Bakersfield. When the 2001 Roadless Rule was established—limiting access through Forest Service lands—he feared access to his mine was jeopardized and Intiso became an activist.

Environmentalists such as those who work at the Klamath-Siskiyou Wild organization, he tells me, want to depopulate rural land and concentrate humans in urban enclaves. "They have maybe an altruistic feeling," he speculates, "that the world would be better if we controlled people more." Anthony Intiso chose to retire in Siskiyou County because he likes the wild country and its self-styled fiercely independent inhabitants. But he's failed to retire. One political cause after another keeps this vibrant campaigner at work, and one of his current projects is to stop vast reaches of his new homeland from becoming a National Monument.

"No Monument!" preaches Anthony Intiso.

A National Monument is defined by the Interior Department as a place of historical or geographical import located on land under jurisdiction of the federal government, and a place subsequently protected by its Monument status. These places are proclaimed National Monuments by the president through the authority granted the White House by the Antiquities Act of 1906. No public hearings are required, no congressional vote. All it takes to make public land administered by the federal government a National Monument is the stroke of a presidential pen back in Washington—and, of course, the political will to do it.[83]

Rough Rider Teddy Roosevelt signed the Antiquities Act into law and proceeded to use its power "to declare by public proclamation" eighteen National Monuments across the West, from the Petrified Forest in Arizona to California's Muir Woods (it's just a few miles from my high school in Mill Valley and I've seen nothing more awe inspiring anywhere) to Mount Olympus in the Pacific Northwest rainforest well north of Jefferson. President Roosevelt expressed his preservationist mentality three years before he signed the Antiquities Act with a speech at the Grand Canyon that reminds us, "Keep this great wonder as it is. You cannot improve it. The ages have been at work on it, and man can only mar it."[84]

Mar it man has along the gaudy south rim approaches from Williams, but the Grand Canyon itself looks as it did before Europeans saw it.

"Proponents of the National Monument have a different philosophy than the farmers and ranchers do," says Intiso. "They come from a mindset that the world would be better off going back to the pre-Columbian era. We believe in another condition." That philosophical conflict, he maintains, is impossible to reconcile. "We're not opposed to preserving something of antiquity that's valuable to our history. That's great. We're not opposed to that at all. In the Antiquities Act it says that the monument cannot exceed five thousand acres." Well, no. I've read the Antiquities Act and it authorizes the president to reserve land for Monuments "the limits of which in all cases shall be confined to the smallest area compatible with proper care and management of the objects to be protected."[85] It says nothing about the five-thousand-acre limit Intiso cites. "That's a lot of land for a Monument," he says about the mythical five thousand acres. "They have taken that law," he says about Klamath-Siskiyou Wild and other environmentalists, "and have gotten the federal government to expand National Monument use to include millions of acres."

Anthony Intiso worries that over six hundred thousand acres in his new neighborhood is in jeopardy of becoming a National Monument. "The border for this proposed Monument comes down to the highway you drove," he says about Highway 96. That would include Rick Jones's store and Bruce Johnson's trailer park. "Within that boundary you have private property. You have people making a living and supporting themselves. They will be removed."

"Or they'll live there until they're dead," I counter, "and their heirs will be bought out by the government."

"They will be removed," he insists, his deep voice booming with the sound of authority that would make him a good candidate for a radio talk show. The language of the Antiquities Act regarding private property is ambiguous and open to interpretation. When the "objects" to be protected "are situated on a tract . . . held in private ownership, the tract, or so much thereof as may be necessary for the proper care and management of the object, may be relinquished to the Government, and the Secretary of the Interior is hereby authorized to accept relinquishment of such tracts in behalf of the Government of the United States."

Whatever the details, Intiso and his colleagues are convinced that the ultimate goal of the proponents of a Monument along the Klamath is to move all the settlers out of the tract in question. "They are lobbying like crazy with the federal government to do that." In addition to the lobbying by private organizations, he tells an example story of federal government harassment of settlers living on lands within the proposed Monument boundaries.

"The Forest Service and the BLM are doing little things to the people who live up there like putting a gate up across the road and locking it so they can't get into their own property. They have to go back to the BLM office in town and say, 'Hey, I need a key.' And the BLM says, 'We'll only let you use it for certain hours.' Come on! Do we believe in private property rights, or don't we?"

Despite all the NO MONUMENT signs, and despite the fierce opposition to creating a National Monument along the Klamath, even those credited with leading the fight against it—like Anthony Intiso—are remarkably uninformed about the status of any pending proposal to designate huge tracts of Jefferson as a National Monument.

"What is its current status?" I ask.

"We don't know," he answers.

"How can you not know? Can't you pick up the phone and call the Interior Department?" Traditional procedure is that the Interior Department recommends to the president that a place become a National Monument.

"They won't tell us! We call them and ask, 'What's going on?' And they say, 'We'll get back to you.' We never hear from them."

"We have to have open space," Intiso says with the passion of a man who discovered Siskiyou County in 1985 and moved north to avoid the urban sprawl of Ventura County. "We can't be developing everything. But we have to manage that open space properly. Do we manage it for the benefit of people or do we manage it for the benefit of animal and vegetation species. Which one do we choose?"

That's doesn't sound to me like a realistic or necessary dichotomy. Just as the old song "Love and Marriage" preaches, "You can't have one without the other." He agrees.

"I don't believe you have to choose either one. I believe in a balanced approach. The Monument does not do that."

"But how can you know if details of any pending Monument proposal and its status in the Interior Department are unknowns?"

"It is total non use by human habitation, period," he is convinced. "That's the ultimate goal of every Monument. No human usage. Why? How does that benefit anybody?"

In fact, just across the California border from where we're talking in Bob's Ranch House Restaurant, over on the Oregon side, a fifty-two-thousand-acre tract of land has been set aside as the Cascade-Siskiyou National Monument ever since President Clinton proclaimed it an "ecological wonder" and an "area of unique geology, biology, climate and topography." But human usage is not prohibited in the Cascade-Siskiyou National Monument, and its borders are a patchwork. Over a third of the land within the Monument's outermost borders is in private hands. Monument lands are used for grazing. They are available for hiking and camping, hunting and fishing, hang gliding, rock climbing, bicycling, and snowmobiling.[86]

"How does that benefit anybody?" Intiso asks rhetorically about his theory that a National Monument is off limits for use by people. Proponents of a National Monument along the Klamath, he tells me, are misguided worshippers of plants and animals other than humans. "It's a religious philosophy that calls for you to worship Mother Earth and believes there is no supreme being that created it all. That's where some of these people," he says about Monument advocates, "are coming from. They don't believe in a supreme being—whatever you want to call it."

"You must worship the Earth, too," I interrupt. "Look out the window." I gesture at the distant mountains on the horizon far from the restaurant where we're meeting. "How can you not worship the Earth? It's gorgeous here."

He concurs, but adds, "I recognize that an ultimate authority— something far greater than us—created it. That creator—whatever it is—created all of this," now it's his turn to recognize the landscape out our window, "for what purpose, to compartmentalize us in a small area and leave the rest of it alone? My logic says no." He says he's not opposed to setting aside some places free from human use but not when such preserves are "harmful to a lot of people. Then it's not a good thing. The Monument," he says with certainty, "will kill what little economy is on the river—completely."

Anthony Intiso and others opposed to the Monument mounted their aggressive public relations campaign (as evidenced by the NO MONUMENT signs lining Highway 96) in an effort to stop it and are poised to go to federal court if the Interior Department requests that the White House use executive power to create the Monument. While they wait for news, they do not know the status of the Monument campaign. Nor does Intiso understand the motives of his opponents.

"Why do they want to harm families?" he says when I solicit questions from him for my upcoming meeting with Monument advocate and lawyer George Sexton, the Klamath-Siskiyou Wild conservation director. "Why do they want to displace people? That's what the Monument status does. When you kill the economy of an area, no matter how small it may be," his voice is rising, and it's clear to me he is passionate about his fears and beliefs, "you kill the people—not literally, but figuratively—displace those people." He estimates four or five thousand people would be adversely affected were the Monument established along the river. "They've got to leave. Why would they want to do that? Why are they motivated to harm other people? That's what they're doing! That's the bottom line."

"I'm a perennial optimist," Anthony Intiso tells me when I ask him if he thinks he and his comrades will prevail in their fight against the Monument. "My Italian nature is I don't give up. I don't give up. Ever. On anything." He's not just Italian. He's a Jeffersonian. "It's our way of life," he says about living in Jefferson. "Open space. Good people. Down to earth. Honest. Handshake agreements. Don't need a damn lawyer to settle a problem." He laughs. He's a lawyer. And, of course, these many years after his move to Jefferson, he and his opponents are well lawyered up, ready to use the courts to fight the dreaded National Monument.

Meanwhile, Anthony Intiso enjoys the romance of Jefferson. He joined other Jeffersonians by buying a stash of newly minted Double XX silver dollars, and he dreams of an economically viable independent state. "We have the natural resources, we're impoverished because they take the money out of the area and they don't send hardly any of it back compared with what they take," he says, echoing the call of the 1941 crowd, and we shake hands.

Chapter Twenty-Seven

SACRED WATER, SACRED LIFE

OVER ON THE McCLOUD RIVER SIDE OF MT. SHASTA, EAST OF ETNA, lie the ancestral lands of the Winnemem Wintu tribe. *Sawal mem, Sawal suhana,* say the Winnemem Wintu about the Jefferson region in their language. Sacred water, sacred life. The tribe sums up its identity and its critical existential challenges with a mission statement: "We are a traditional tribe who inhabits our ancestral territory from Mt. Shasta down the McCloud River watershed. When the Shasta Dam was constructed during World War II, it flooded our home and blocked the salmon runs. The salmon are an integral part of our lifeway and of a healthy McCloud River watershed. We believe that when the last salmon is gone, humans will be gone too. Our fight to return the salmon to the McCloud River is no less than a fight to save the Winnemem Wintu Tribe."

I meet with a chief and spiritual leader of the tribe, Caleen Sisk, a woman with a warm, wide smile and welcoming eyes. She was wearing a traditional basket hat. "It honors one of our staple food sources, which is the acorn. The acorns have caps. So the women who carry on our traditions wear the basket caps." Patterns on the cap, she tells me, represent mountains, quail, deer, and hunters. Wives of hunters wear such caps to signify that the quail and deer their men bring home are not just for their immediate family. "We don't have starving people in the villages."

Her hair is separated into two long braids and around her neck is a dentalia necklace—made from seashells. "This is from our ocean people," she explains to me. "It signifies where our salmon come from, and that we worry, and that we have songs. We have songs for the salmon that are in the ocean as well as the salmon coming up the rivers." When the Shasta Dam was built across the McCloud River, Winnemem Wintu lands were flooded, territory the tribe says the federal government promised to replace. The promises, say the tribe, were forgotten and—to add to the injury—in 1985 Washington ceased recognizing the tribe as American Indians, ending their special federal benefits as Native Americans. No official

Winnemem Wintu chief Caleen Sisk under a traditional basket cap.
Courtesy Marc Dadigan

government status as Indians means it is illegal for the tribe's chiefs to possess eagle feathers for ritual use. The tribe's students cannot take advantage of Bureau of Indian Affairs scholarships. Language restoration funding is denied the tribe. The list of opportunities no longer available to the tribe is long.[87]

When we talk, Chief Sisk figures the Winnemem Wintu number around 125, down from a population estimated by her as upwards of fifteen thousand when contact was first made with encroaching settlers. Numbers continue to dwindle, she says, as some Winnemem Wintu use their close relationships with the recognized Pit River tribe and become Pit River Indians in order to take advantage of opportunities only available to recognized tribes.

"No one should have to do that," she laments about the abandonment, because it dilutes cultures.

Her conflict is not with Jefferson or with Sacramento or with Salem; it's with Washington. "We're fighting for the salmon. We're fighting to return the salmon to the McCloud River." And the tribe is fighting to use land they consider sacred for tribal ceremonies. They want to close a small patch of public land to non–Winnemem Wintu, for example, during the few days a year of what they call their Puberty Ceremony—when girls swim across the McCloud to become women while the tribe dances and prays. Chief Sisk insists such rituals should take place absent white anglers fishing on the nearby riverbanks coincidently witnessing the ceremony—and sometimes heckling participants.

She puts such conflict into context quoting testimony her great-grandmother gave Congress. "What gives the white people the right to come here and kill my people, to take our homes away and treat us so badly? Our blood is the same as other human beings. We are people, too. Just because the color of my skin is brown it doesn't give them more rights than the creator put down for all people. I'm trying to make the white men see that the sacred spring on Mt. Shasta— the herbal medicines and the spiritual doctoring we use to heal our people—are connected. It is not something that can be separated. Our children will need our religious ways, our language, our sacred places to call themselves Wintu Indians in the future."

Chief Caleen Sisk straddles the two worlds. An educator, she studied at Chico State University (arguably located in Jefferson) and then returned to the California Central Valley campus to work for several years recruiting Indian students to come to Chico State to study. Were Jefferson a separate state, she worries, life for the Winnemem

Wintu might be more troublesome than it is for them as Californians. "We're fighting for different things," she says about the Indians and white settlers. She cites conflicts between campers and the tribe's use of sacred sites. "Tradition and culture are our driving forces, not economics, and we're not willing to give up."

The chief launches into a passionate speech to explain her worries not just for the tribe, but for life itself. "Once they ruin all the water nobody lives on, nothing lives on. I don't think people realize how many rivers have been polluted. People have to wake up right now. They have to stop chasing the American dream of being rich." She identifies one of the villains. "It's the off-road vehicles—the big boys' toys—polluting the rivers and lakes. Our biggest job is to continue being who we are. We have watched as they took all the lumber, all the trees. They took all the gold from the rivers and no longer look for it except for a hobby. Now they're taking all the oil—everywhere. Everything they can find, they're taking all of it. They have destroyed mountains by mining. But we're still here. We're still singing. And our biggest job right now is to bring the salmon back. And if we can bring the salmon back . . ." she stops at that dream to explain how the tribe hopes to make it come true.

Next I am surprised by a most fantastic story. Years ago, the chief tells me, some McCloud River salmon eggs were sent to New Zealand. They hatched in an isolated river that now supports a population of salmon with McCloud roots. Winnemem Wintu traveled across the Pacific and met with Maori tribesmen who agreed to reciprocate. The Maori offered eggs to the Indians so that they could repopulate their California river with McCloud salmon descendants. The unique McCloud salmon disappeared when the Shasta Dam was built in the 1940s and blocked the fish's spawning run. The federal government intends to build a passage around the dam for spawning salmon and instead of embracing efforts to repopulate the McCloud with salmon found downstream in the Sacramento River, the Winnemem Wintu want to bring home the McCloud salmon. "They're diseased and exposed to mining poisons," Chief Sisk says about Sacramento River salmon. "The McCloud is still pristine. It's pure. It's cold. It's like it was when they left."

The Winnemem Wintu creation myth is intertwined with salmon. "When we first bubbled out of our sacred spring on Mt. Shasta at the time of creation we were helpless and unable to speak," is tribal lore. "It was salmon, the Nur, who took pity on us and gave us their voice. In return, we promised always to speak for them."[88]

Before we part, Caleen Sisk, who is both chief and spiritual leader, shares a sacred Winnemem Wintu song with me. It's an almost monotonic chant that she sings with what sounds to me like a humble and ritualistic voice. She translates the hymn for me: "Only the Creator is our teacher/We only learn from the Creator/We know this because the Creator sent that message to us/I know this in my heart/It'll always be, as long as I can sing."

Chapter Twenty-Eight

Media Free-for-All

JEFFERSON PUBLIC RADIO ISN'T THE ONLY MEDIA OUTLET USING the Jefferson moniker as its identity. The web-based State of Jefferson podcast wraps itself in the Jefferson legacy. Run by a couple of friends in Eureka, California, the podcast's website homepage features a quote attributed to Thomas Jefferson: "I think myself that we have more machinery of government than is necessary, too many parasites living on the labor of the industrious." Jefferson was such a prolific writer during his long lifetime that it seems quotes can be pulled from his works to support just about any point of view. Phil Elcock and Josh Payne created the podcast with the goal of "turning a state of mind into a state of reality," as they proclaim from the site's homepage. I caught up with them in Elcock's living room via Skype. Payne and Elcock see themselves as carrying on the heritage of the 1941 Jefferson "revolt," because, as Payne tells me, "We are out in BFE Nowhere. What we require from our government doesn't apply to what people in Sacramento need."

Of course. And Bakersfield is worried about water while Santa Cruz is concerned about urban sprawl. Calexico's crises regarding the Mexican border differ from Lake Tahoe's. Street crime dominates civic debate in Oakland while in Santa Barbara local political chatter over coffee more likely deals with offshore oil drilling. California is diverse. So is Oregon. Cowboys out on the high Oregon northeast around Pendleton worry about their cattle while waitresses at hipster Portland eateries on Alberta Street show off their vibrant whole sleeve tattoos. The fish boat crews in Newport spend off seasons repairing crab pots and talking fisheries policy while a few hours down Highway 101 on the golf course in Bandon the gossip is about handicaps. In Eugene, Ducks football is Topic A while in barren southeast Oregon alkali basins, ducks are for hunting.

That diversity is exactly why Jefferson should secede, says Elcock. "We think it's a better idea to break the states up because one government can't satisfy everybody. That's one of the reasons why our Founders decided to make this country a union of states, because of the different cultures, different geographical areas, and different types of people who want a government that represents them the best. When you have one government that represents everybody, nobody is going to be satisfied."

Elcock and Payne see their version of the Jefferson dream as an opportunity to, as Elcock says, "reduce the size of government and put responsibility back into the hands of the people." But Payne accepts limits on localizing government. "When does it become impractical?" he asks. "Every town has a wealthy part and a poor part," he offers as an example. "The needs at opposite ends of a small town are drastically different. I don't have the answer to when it becomes impractical buffoonery."

With his Fu Manchu moustache, black T-shirt, and shaved head, Phil Elcock could dress in Gold Rush–era fashions and look like he belonged in nineteenth-century Eureka. He places himself back in yesteryear when he explains how his vision of Jefferson could do without even basic government services. "A lot of it could be done through volunteer work. I advocate privatization of police. That's kind of the way it was done back in the early 1800s when neighborhoods and communities would band together and watch out for each other." He offers private security companies as contemporary iterations of those good old days while I'm contemplating the Old West vigilantes who took the law into their own hands, often terrorizing their communities and stringing up the wrong man after acting as self-appointed cop and judge. "Why not let them compete against law enforcement agencies?" he says about the private guards. "I think you would get better service for a cheaper cost because you could stop paying them. We can't stop paying our taxes, not without having our doors kicked in and being arrested. Government services could be a lot more efficient if they had to compete for our business. Does that make sense?"

Not much. Now I'm thinking about the expanding privatization of American prisons, a phenomenon I encountered when I was researching my book, *The Dangerous World of Butterflies*. The self-described "world's most wanted butterfly smuggler" was being held in a federal prison in California. The longstanding procedure for journalists who want to get inside the walls to conduct a jailhouse interview with a federal prisoner is to obtain approval from the inmate and the warden. But private prisons add another factor: final approval from corporate headquarters. That means for-profit companies are allowed to dictate who conducts oversight of a crucial element of society's criminal justice system.

Podcaster Josh Payne is not in lockstep with his partner about private police patrolling Jefferson. "Privatization of government services lends itself to a lack of transparency," he says, "a first step to corruption."

The duo produces a podcast every Thursday and tally between two and three hundred listeners a month. Both raised in Eureka, they vamp about what they think a State of Jefferson should be, based on a shared belief that Oregon, California, and the federal government are all "broken," and that Jefferson is a natural place to start the repairs because of its longstanding sense of regional identity. The show makes them no money. They hope their few ads will at least pay for the Internet hosting charges and their equipment costs. Only a few hundred listeners a month mean not enough to attract many advertising dollars. Their business balance sheet reflects Jefferson's. Residents of the proposed state can complain about Sacramento and Salem all they want, but Sacramento and Salem pay Jefferson's bills.

Secession is unlikely anytime soon, Elcock and Payne know, but Elcock thinks incremental steps toward greater local autonomy are possible, and that a Jefferson region could become a viable entity without statehood, starting with locals "telling California and Oregon, 'Hey, your laws are too encroaching and too invasive on our personal liberties here.' Legally, of course," he says about such a revolt. "We never advocate violent revolution. That's wrong. We already have a stereotype up here of being gun-toting rednecks. We don't need to perpetuate that."

Although neither truly expects Jefferson will ever become the 51st state, they refuse to call secession impossible. "You never know. One can dream," says Elcock. "The more people yell about it, talk about it," says Payne, "the more likely it is to happen. In a century, if it does happen, they'll look back to the beginnings of the State of Jefferson and they'll see the folks in the forties on the roads with the rifles, they'll see our little podcast. We'll get to be a step in the process; whether it happens or not is anybody's guess. It's definitely something worth working towards."

On the podcast homepage the authors define their goals. "It makes no sense to have laws and regulations dictated to us by city dwellers what [sic] have little to no knowledge of rural living and the needs and concerns that come with it," they write. "Those of us that live in the nineteen counties that make up the rural State of Jefferson continue to be ignored in favor of the big cities that out number us in voting power. Instead of enjoying the representation we deserve as hard working and tax paying Californians and Oregonians, we constantly see our liberties, our jobs and our wealth stripped from us in return for more intrusive laws, stifling regulations, suffocating government and more taxes and fees. Unless Salem and Sacramento listens [sic] to our plight, our only other recourse is to carve out a

new state where self-governance, just courts, freedom from government intrusion and prosperity can flourish once again."[89] The team
needs a copy editor. From our conversation I know they do not mean
that they seek freedom from prosperity.

The podcast offers links to Liz Bowen's Pie N Politics blog, State
of Jefferson.com, and to the State of Jefferson Party Facebook page.

StateofJefferson.com is the work of former logger Brian Peterson. On
the site he reproduces the "Proclamation of Independence" and has
sold Jeffersonian memorabilia like T-shirts and Jefferson-XX flags.
Government restrictions on Pacific Northwest logging operations
help stimulate his secessionist tendencies. "It just goes to show that
we're still being double crossed," is how he interprets current forest
conservation rules and regulations. "We're just not being represented
here. We don't have the voice and the votes. If we had our own state,
we'd have more control over our destiny and the laws that are made."[90]

I borrowed my wife's secret code so I could study Jefferson on
Facebook. I closed my own account years ago because Facebook is so
annoying. The State of Jefferson Party Facebook page is named Jefferson State. So—as an example of what's annoying—Facebook asks
me, "Do you know Jefferson?" Facebook is on a first name basis with
Mr. State. "If you know Jefferson," the scheming company orders me,
"send him a friend request."

Behind the Facebook page is Charles William Walker. He posts
prompts to generate responses from Jefferson's friends, prompts
such as this one from September 29, 2012: "If North Dakota has an
unemployment rate of 3.5%, shouldn't Oregon and California be
looking at why it is so low and apply it? Oh, wait. We don't do the
common sense and logical thing. Which is why we need our own
state!" Friends of Jefferson commented immediately.

Michelle pointed out, "North Dakota has an oil boom going on right now."

But Shawn countered with, "Yea, a buddy of mine just got back, said it was booming up in Fargo. He couldn't take the winters lol even for a job lol. Love the state of Jefferson."

Jerome checked in with "It's time to suceed [*sic*]." Hard to tell if he meant that Jeffersonians need success or should secede.

Jesse added to the brainstorming with a list of Jefferson's economic assets. "Logging, Mining, Water, Weed. Does anyone reading this have any comprehension as to how much cash money is brought into northern California and southern Oregon because of the marijuana industry? It would blow your mind. California is dependent on Jefferson. Their laws effect [*sic*] us and we send them taxes, but we sure don't get much back."

In fact, Jesse, you get millions of dollars more back into Jefferson than you send down to Sacramento, according to Kristin Shelton, Program Budget Manager in the California Department of Finance. She and her staff were gracious enough to take time away from their routine work to analyze Jefferson tax income and government expenditures (on the California side of the border) for me. I sent her the study conducted in 1941 by her predecessor, Fred W. Binks, then chief of the California Department of Finance Division of Budgets and Accounts, and asked her to compile a 2013 equivalent based on figures from the 2011 to 2012 fiscal year. "All things considered," concluded Mr. Binks back in 1941, "the 'State of Jefferson' has made a rather good fiscal deal, whether the people there know it or not."

That fiscal deal still looks rather good.

"As you requested," Ms. Shelton wrote, "we have put together an estimate of the state revenues that are derived from and the state expenditures that are expended on the four counties that would have comprised the 'state of Jefferson.' As you will see from the attached spreadsheet, we estimate that these four counties contribute about $168.3 million in revenue to the state of California and that the state of California, in turn, spends about $188.5 million on programs within these four counties." Her office's estimates were based only on what she identified as "the largest state program areas."

That means about $20 million more is shipped north than comes back to the capital each year. The spreadsheet Ms. Shelton attached lists income, corporate, alcohol and tobacco taxes on the revenue side for the state, along with regulatory fees. The costs Sacramento assumes are dominated by education: Over $150 million is sent north to fund the kindergarten through twelfth grade schooling for Jefferson children. Over $25 million is spent on prisons and rehabilitation, just under $7 million is budgeted for health and other citizen services (*not* including Medi-Cal, the state's Medicare program), and a mere $3 million goes to the prime rebel yell of the 1941 secessionists: roads.

In fact, Jefferson's 2013 deal with Sacramento looks not just good, but great.

The magic of the Internet expanded Jefferson citizenship worldwide. Anonymous Toni checked into the Jefferson State Facebook page acknowledging she had never been to Oregon or California. "I just believe that people should have local level rights and I sympathize with y'alls position of being pushed between two liberal nanny states. Good luck with y'alls endeavors!"

In a rambling YouTube video presentation linked to the Facebook page, founder Charles Walker, wearing a red T-shirt and sitting in a dark room, explains five routes he thinks Jefferson can take to become a state. A political party (like his, he says) could work to elect local politicians in California and Oregon who would put referendums on ballots in both states. Citizens of both states could sign petitions for statehood. "We could sue California and Oregon for basically violating their constitutions because if a state violates its own constitution it's an illegal government, which," he looks for words off camera, "is an interesting thought." His fourth and fifth routes call for devolution of Jefferson into a territory and then an application for statehood, or two territories—one out of each state "in case there is a hiccup with the northern part."

The Constitution of the United States, not Charles Walker's haphazard research and brainstorming, is of course the ultimate arbiter of how a state is formed. Article IV, Section 3 of the Constitution is clear and specific. "No new State shall be formed or erected within the Jurisdiction of any other state; nor any State be formed by the Junction of two or more States, or Parts of States, without the Consent of the Legislatures of the States concerned as well as of the Congress."

Under harsh lighting that makes his baby face seem both innocent and megalomaniacal, and with an American flag on display stage left, Walker tries to establish an aura of authority based on a scattered collection of anti–big government ideas and a patchwork understanding of Jefferson's history. "What I've been thinking about," he tells his four-hundred-plus followers, "is how this stuff can happen." His delivery is sweetly sincere and often confused.

"It's kind of a minority geographic-wise and population-wise in Oregon," Walker—a Klamath Falls native—says about the part of Jefferson in Oregon that he worries might be a hiccup. "But I think at this point Oregon is pretty much one of those states where it hates being itself. You got the southern part that doesn't like the northern part. You got the eastern part that doesn't like the western part. With all the crap going on in the country, I'm sure a lot of southern

Oregonians and eastern Oregonians don't want Portland, Eugene, and Salem controlling their lives."

His eyes open wider and he pleads, "I need more of you people talking to me, 'cause a lot of you people out there have been slackin'. I'm just going to point that out right now. We need every Jeffersonian being enthusiastic. Congress said we could be a state December 1941. Pearl Harbor happened. Boom. They unplugged us. We were a state for four days. We elected John C. Childs to be our governor." He raises his hands, moves in on the camera, and raises his voice. "We had a governor!" He bashes the table with his fists. "For four days!" He reaches over to adjust the camera in case it bounced when he hit the table. "So quit slacking, Jeffersonians!" He points at the camera. "We were there! And we need to get back there! I hope this inspires you all." He waves at the camera, and says, "Bye!"

Charles Walker ranting about southern Oregonians and eastern Oregonians not wanting Portland, Eugene, and Salem controlling their lives enjoys years of precedent, including an editorial in the *Medford Mail* back in 1909. "Narrow-visioned mossbacks" who "exert most of their energy in blocking progress" it called the citizens of Oregon's major cities. "With eastern Oregon seceding on the one hand and southern Oregon on the other," as the paper advocated with tongue in cheek, "the Willamette Valley will be left peacefully to vegetate by itself and the Salem hog and the Portland pig can root undisturbed among the pest-laden orchards, wallow in the streaks of mire called roads, drink Arbuckle coffee and read the *Oregonian*."[91]

Chapter Twenty-Nine

THERE'S GOLD IN THAT THERE RIVER

JUST A FEW BLOCKS OFF I-5 IN GRANTS PASS, A NONDESCRIPT CONCRETE block building with bars on the windows is home to the Armadillo Mining Shop. Signs out front promise NEW & USED MINING EQUIPMENT, and specifically PANS SLUICES DREDGES. An American flag is waving in the hot afternoon breeze. I've come to the Armadillo to meet its proprietor Robert Stumbo and to hear a sales pitch for the state-of-the-art suction dredges he sells.

"The water gets sucked up this hose into the high-pressure pump." Stumbo is explaining how the dredge works. We're studying at a unit made by Keene Engineering ("Dedicated to providing you with the finest mining and prospecting equipment for over 50 years!") that goes for about $2300. It's a contraption that looks to me like a go-kart with pontoons hooked up to a vacuum cleaner. When the dredge is floating, water and rocks are sucked up off the creek or riverbed and the rocks are scattered into the sluice box. "In the sluice box all the bigger rocks go right back out and into the river. The water goes right back into the river. Your heavy material—the gold and a lot of lead that we pick out of the river—goes through this grate down to these mats down there and sticks on those mats." The gold drops to the mats because its weight separates it from the water as it flows through the sluice box. "Everything else goes right back into the river almost down where you got it from." The dredge is about six feet long. The rocks and water it sucks up get dumped back into the river about six feet from where they were removed by the machine. "At the end of the day you shut the machine off. You take the grates out and you take those carpets out," he says about the mats, "and rinse them out." If you're lucky, there's gold—flakes and little nuggets—in them there rugs. If you're really lucky, there are bigger nuggets that you can pick off the mats before you start the rinse job.

Miners tend to wear wet suits and scuba gear when they operate the suction dredges in the river water; it runs cold year-round in Jefferson. "They're under water, running the suction hose. If you're in any water that's deeper than your arm is long, you have to go under water. If you're working hard, you can't hold your breath long enough. It's easier to have an air supply." The dredges are equipped with air compressors to keep the miners supplied with air.

The dredge engines purr quietly, Stumbo tells me, so he rejects the idea that noise pollution generated by the miners destroys the tranquility of the Jefferson wilderness. "Someone is camped along the river and someone else is downriver a ways running a suction dredge. Cars are going by on the road. They never say anything about the cars and trucks going by on the road, but they just hate that miner down there."

"How about the guy in the next campsite with the super-annoying music cranked up loud?" I add from my own memories of disturbed paradises.

"Yeah," says Stumbo, "that's okay, but that miner? Damn him. Noise pollution is just another excuse. We've got jet airplanes flying over here day and night."

"What about the stink from the exhaust?"

"With these new engines," he points to the Keene, "it's no different than your car. There's very little emission smell."

All that gear doesn't come cheap. But the combination of a tough job market and a hefty gold price attracts miners who Stumbo says are not hobbyists; they're earning their living in the river. And if they've doing it legally as of 2012, they must confine their operations on the Rogue River to two and a half summer months.

The thought of pulling a fortune—or even just a living—out of the river is compelling. I can feel the lure, wandering around the store looking at the dredges and pans and other mining paraphernalia on offer. Stumbo adds to that lure and the romance with the tempting line, "If you hit a rich streak in the river, you can make a thousand bucks a day." But he tempers my gold fever with his next line. "If you don't hit a rich streak in the river, you can make ten dollars a day."

"Or less after you buy the gasoline for the dredge," I figure.

"Or less," he agrees with a realistic laugh. "It all depends on your mining ability. You go out to the river and you test spots until finally you hit one where it starts paying. The way the river lays this gold in there—they call them pay streaks—once you hit one of these, you can follow it. Sometimes they go a few feet, sometimes they go quite a ways, and you can work right up this pay streak." As an example of what might be under the water, he points me to a photograph of a four-ounce nugget one of his customers took out of the Rogue River. When I go over to the counter to take a look at the picture, I'm distracted by a burly, bearded mountain man who looks as if he just came in from gold digging and as if he hasn't bathed or changed his clothes for weeks. He's sitting on a stool showing off a nugget about the size and shape of a small lima bean to the clerk behind the counter, hoping to get a good price from Stumbo, who buys gold from miners for 75 percent of the daily spot price.

"Where did you find it?" I ask the miner.

"Placer mining." This was a fellow of few words who expressed no interest in getting to know me better. I've lived in the rural West long enough to recognize that his grunted reply, along with the irritated look on his face, made it clear we weren't likely to become beer-drinking buddies.

"Placer mining," I respond. "Where?"

Stumbo's clerk interrupts. "There ya go," she says, "that was the answer you're gonna get."

"That's it?" I say to my volunteer interpreter.

"That was it," she affirms. "You ask them more than that and you'll offend them." She talks about my mountain man as if he represents all the miners out in the hills who are working their dream alone. She's probably correct. "They are very particular that way."

Mountain man sits, looks at his gold, and stays mum.

"It looks fine to me," Stumbo tells her, after he inspects the gold and the fresh scratches she's etched in the nugget. (Later he tells me that he's confident from his years of mining experience that he knows what's a solid gold nugget and what's a fraud. "People make fake nuggets with lead that they beat up and cover with a layer of gold.") The clerk weighs it and it comes to 2.63 DWT. That's its dram weight; a dram is $\frac{1}{16}$ of an ounce. The spot gold price this day is $1732.60; mountain man leaves Armadillo mining with $170.87 in his dirty pants pocket.

Robert Stumbo is a stocky man with silver hair. He tells me he tends to use a loupe when he's assessing gold these days—his eyes aren't what they were. He strikes me as a good salesman, and he knows the business from both sides—he's done some mining over the years himself. "It was okay, but it's just not my cup of tea." He doesn't promise buying the equipment packed into his store means you'll strike it rich. But I see how his enthusiasm for miners' dreams is contagious even when he warns against counting those nuggets before they're found. "When you see that yellow stuff in there, it gets your old pumper going." He beats his chest and his eyes widen. "But we tell everybody right up front that you might not get anything. We don't tell them that they're going to go out and get rich. We tell them the first year you're probably not going to find anything." This kind of one-man mining seems like grueling and tough work.

"It's like being a cowboy or being a logger or being a police-man or whatever else." Stumbo understands what sends men into the river. "It's what's in your blood. It's like driving trucks. I've got a truck-driving license. It does nothing for me. But there are other people who live and die to drive a truck. Mining is the same. If you hit a good streak, the rewards can be great." Stumbo rejects the term hobbyist to define his customers. "Trust me, buddy. If you're out there working hard, you're fairly serious. Mining is not easy. You do not go out there and just find it, except maybe in rare occasions. You've got to shovel and pick. It's backbreaking labor. Even panning, you're digging in the rocks and you're moving rocks. You're on your hands and knees working hard all day."

Robert Stumbo's personal Oregon history goes back genera-tions. "Born and raised here. I think my first relatives were here in the 1850s. I know this part of the state well and I'm proud of it. We've been mining on these rivers for close to two hundred years and everybody says our rivers are pristine and beautiful. Where's the harm?" The same goes for the mountainsides, he insists. "They say our forests are beautiful. Wait a minute. We've been managing our forests. Most of them are second and third growth; some were planted by my grandfather. They don't understand that we need to use the earth to make our living." The "they" he's talking about are environmental activists and government officials who want to stop mining and logging. "They're destroying people's lives and it needs to be addressed."

He adds the Karuk tribe to his list of adversaries. "They take thousands and thousands of salmon out of the river every year, gill netting them. But they're always talking about the coho salmon being rare. The coho salmon weren't native to the Klamath River. They were introduced. They're talking about these native species, but they're not native. The rest of the salmon are doing fine." Stumbo rejects claims that suction mining hurts salmon spawning grounds.

"That's hooey, to put it politely." The river moves tons of rock downstream. "Our little bit of turbidity we make with a suction dredge is not harming the fish."

There is no science to prove mining harms the river that he's seen, Stumbo says. He cites racism for the Karuk tribe's push to remove miners from Jefferson rivers. "Those Indians don't like the white people. They were quoted in one of their meetings saying they were going to use the salmon as their spotted owl to run all the white men off the river and give it all back to the Indians. Now if I was to go down there and say we're going to get rid of all these Indians, I would be a racist and a criminal. I'd get it for a hate crime. Yet they can do this stuff wantonly. They're a gang of thugs. They're a bunch of people who have declared themselves a club, a tribe, and they're going out there and destroying other people's livelihoods."

"But they have a history here that even predates the long one of your family."

Of course, says Stumbo. "And I agree there should be concessions to them to a certain extent because of that." He takes a breath, flashes a smile, and adds, "But if it wasn't for us poor old white boys, they'd either be talking Japanese or German."

"There were Indians fighting against the Axis," I remind him.

"Yes there were," he agrees. "My dad fought with a little Indian guy from Chiloquin. They stayed together through most of the Philippines and New Guinea."

"Yet with all this shared history, I hear some extraordinarily inflammatory language from the parties at odds here."

"And it's too bad it has to come to that." Stumbo pauses and says he wants to choose his words carefully. "The Indians got treated badly. Nobody is going to argue with that. But I didn't do anything to those Indians. My dad didn't do anything to Indians. I doubt if his dad did. But my great-great-grandfather, maybe he had some trouble with the Indians. How long are we going to have to pay for what happened 150 years ago? We need to move on. If they want a little piece of ground to call their ancestral home, hey, there you go. Be happy. Be well. Prosper." His tone is a taste supercilious; however it doesn't sound insincere. "But they don't want that. They want to destroy most of what we are. At what point do *our* history and *our* heritage come into it? And if you want to go back far enough, the Karuk Indians and all the rest of those Indians were fighting each other tooth and nail for thousands of years. Where do you stop the wars?"

I tell him about my conversation with Karuk biologist Ken Brink and his belief that nothing should be allowed to disturb the coho because the endangered fish are of supreme importance on the river. Stumbo says the Endangered Species Act calls for trying our best to protect endangered species "and I believe we should."

"You eat salmon?" I ask him.

"You bet! We should protect these species. But if push comes to shove, and something's got to go, sayonara salmon."

Sayonara Salmon. It sounds like a good name for a punk band.

"I don't want to see that happen, and nobody does. They're not in danger of going extinct," he claims. "We're having record salmon runs here on the Rogue River."

Before we say sayonara to each other, I ask Robert Stumbo about Jefferson as a potential 51st state. Not a chance he says. "Them boys is long gone," he says about 1941 conspirators. "I think the Jefferson spirit is still here because all of rural Oregon is ruled by Portland-Salem-Eugene, and they care not for us. They sit up there and they don't seem to realize where their food comes from, where their lumber and the gravel for their nice streets come from. 'Where do you get your food?'" He questions an imaginary Portlander. "'I get it at Safeway,'" he provides the answer. "'No,'" he tells the fantasy urbanite, "'You don't realize that a truck brings that and puts it in that store for you.' We're their bread and butter. We keep this state running. We support them up there."

It's a long good-bye. Stumbo keeps talking. He wants me to know that he expects ultimately to lose the battle with those who want to close down suction dredge mining on the Oregon side of the border, but not without a fight. When I note that he and his clientele seem like they're enjoying themselves, he compares his and his comrades' plight to "the guys at the Alamo." He laughs. "They probably were all sitting around having a drink thinking, 'What are we gonna do? Well, we'll just do what we can. We'll shoot 'em up a little bit and see what happens.'" But the jocular tone changes before I leave. "It's bad," he says. "We're losing our land. We're losing our country. It's terrifying and it makes you madder than hell. America senses it. That's why everybody is buying the hell out of guns and bullets."

Chapter Thirty

WHERE IT ALL BEGAN

I LEAVE THE ARMADILLO MINING SHOP AND HEAD INTO DOWNTOWN Grants Pass, rolling under the IT'S THE CLIMATE sign that arches over the main drag. Today the weather *is* perfect, sunny and warm. But I've been here during miserable wet and cold winters when that sign looks like a not-very-funny joke. I cross the Rogue River thinking about the gold nuggets still to be found and how easy it could be to succumb to gold fever. That little nugget I saw traded for cash—not quite the size of an M&M—picked out of the river and worth a couple of hundred dollars!

I wind down Highway 238 through the Rogue Valley, past signs offering fresh-picked berries for sale and eggs from chickens ranging free, on to Jacksonville. On California Street I sit myself down on a bench and study the red brick United States Hotel across the street. Built in 1880, it is elegantly restored and for sale for just under a million and a half dollars. The United States Hotel sits on the site of what was the Union Hotel, the locale where a meeting called by the *Yreka Herald* "for the purpose of taking into consideration the propriety of organizing a new territory (to be called Jackson), and to devise means to effect the same" occurred on January 7, 1854.[92] Long before Jefferson there was Jackson.

On this summer evening, the nineteenth-century buildings lining the few blocks of downtown Jacksonville sparkle. Except for the automobiles and the tourists, it's easy for me to sit on the bench

The Jacksonville site of the initial 1854 separatists' meeting.

and daydream, imagining the movers-and-shakers back in 1854 at a boisterous gathering, resolved to carve their own political entity out of their piece of Oregon and California. They agreed on language for a protest to Congress, part of their campaign to create Jackson Territory. "Resolved," they wrote, "that we will use every exertion to prevent the formation of a state government in Oregon with its present boundaries."[93]

A leading Oregon politician at the time was General Joseph Lane. Lane was territorial governor and Oregon's delegate to Congress. His son-in-law, Lafayette Mosher, presided over the Jackson Territory organizing meeting. But General Lane was a pragmatist and he refused to back the Jackson movement. The general, who earned his stars fighting in the Mexican-American War, was a southern transplant to the Pacific Northwest. Son-in-law Mosher was an alleged member of the Western Division of the Knights of the Golden Circle,[94] a secret society that promoted slavery.[95] The combination of Lane's southern roots and slavery sympathies fueled fears that the Jacksonites wanted to create a slave state on the West Coast. General Lane worried that the Jackson Territory campaign would interfere with his grander goal of statehood for the Oregon Territory. The natives who lived on and from the land the settlers were mining were harassing gold prospectors along the Rogue River, and armed conflicts between settlers and natives distracted the early separatists. The Jackson Territory faded to black.

General Lane saddled up his warhorse once again and led volunteers in the vicious Rogue River Indian Wars of 1855 and 1856. He was wounded in the battle of Evans Creek, "felled by a Minié ball in his right shoulder." Several hours later the Rogues fighting Lane's volunteers yelled for a ceasefire. Lane, along with interpreters, met them on the battlefield and the two sides scheduled talks. "The Indians, as soon as our firing ceased," wrote one of Lane's soldiers later, "carried out water to our wounded men, and furnished a party to assist in conveying the litters with our wounded for 25 miles, through the mountains."[96] Treaty talks presided over by Lane a couple of weeks after the battle resulted in the Rogue River Indians agreeing to peace in exchange for their land. The Indians were granted a temporary reservation on the north side of the Rogue. That peace ended when white settlers fighting under a flag labeled with the word EXTERMINATION, and who called themselves the "Exterminators," surprise attacked one of the Indian camps, killing about two dozen men, women, and children. The massacre—led by a settler named James Lupton—provoked the final battles of the Rogue River Indian Wars. Lupton died at the scene, an arrow through his lungs.[97] His legacy: The cowardly assault and murders are known to history as Lupton's Massacre. Indians retaliated, but eventually were outgunned. The white settlers were reinforced when a platoon of Army soldiers joined the fight. Those soldiers were not expecting to fight in what became the toughest battle of the Rogue River wars. They were a detail of engineers, assigned to carve a route through the rugged coast range from Port Orford to the inland Applegate Trail—the beginnings of the bad Jefferson roads Mayor Gilbert Gable was campaigning to improve with his initial call for secession. Known as the Battle of Hungry Hill, the location of the pivotal fight was confirmed by Southern Oregon University archaeologists in late 2012 when field work uncovered unfired .69-caliber musket balls of the type that were used in the Springfield muskets issued to Army dragoons in 1855.[98] The Rogue River Indian Wars finally ended when the indigenous tribes that lived around Jacksonville were forced far from their ancestral homelands—the ur-Jefferson—and off to a reservation west of Salem.[99]

When Oregon became a state in 1859, its borders included Jacksonville and one of its first two senators was Joseph Lane. His Oregon political career collapsed after he unsuccessfully ran for vice president of the United States in 1860 on a pro-slavery ticket with presidential candidate John C. Breckenridge. Lane's term in the Senate ended in 1861 and he moved home to Roseburg, along the Umpqua River, on the northern border of most Jefferson maps.[100]

The Oregon county where I live is Lane County. Lane County—headquarters of the University of Oregon, with a growing Mexican community, famous for its alternative lifestyles dating back to the 1960s, where Ken Kesey and the Merry Pranksters painted their bus Further, and where the Lane County Historical Museum hosts the recurring exhibit called *Tie Dye & Tofu: How Mainstream Eugene Became a Counterculture Haven*—is named after a Mexico-invading and Indian-fighting warrior from the South who advocated and promoted slavery. Despite his pedigree, Lane—were he to come back to Oregon—might pass for a local in Eugene's counterculture headquarters, the Whiteaker District (named for Oregon's first governor). The old soldier was described by a reporter for the *Oregon Statesman*: "His hair so twisted, tangled and matted that it would have frightened the teeth out of a curry comb, and set all tonsorial operations at defiance, was surmounted by the remains of an old forage cap, which, judging from its appearance, might have been worn at Braddock's defeat."[101] That sounds as if he looked like a contemporary dreadlocked Whiteaker local boy, dressed in Army surplus.

I rise from the Jacksonville sidewalk bench and stroll California Street admiring the old storefronts, romanticizing those good old days. A closer look at what is now the Bella Union Restaurant and Saloon reveals a plaque identifying it as the F.A. Stewart Building, built in 1970 by Universal Studios for the filming of *The Great Northfield Minnesota Raid*, a reminder of how distorted and deceiving reality is, especially at first glance.

Chapter Thirty-One

DRINKING WITH THE GREENIES

THE CONSERVATION ORGANIZATION KNOWN AT K-S WILD, KLAMATH-Siskiyou Wildlands Center, is headquartered in Ashland. Their mission statement is broad and simple: "Protecting the wild places of northern California and southern Oregon." The detailed K-S Wild literature is specific. It says its experts monitor and influence federal management of millions of acres of forest, work that's "kept tens of thousands of acres of native forests, standing and has helped restore previously logged and fire suppressed stands throughout the region." K-S Wild is proud of its work protecting wildlife and wildlife habitat. That includes not only the contentious debate about water and coho salmon, but also the famous *Strix occidentalis caurina*, an animal most of us know better by its common name, northern spotted owl. K-S Wild figures that it is now the best-known species in America because when it was added to the endangered species list, indiscriminate logging in the Pacific Northwest came to end. But conservationists say the fight is not over. "KS Wild has been challenging and litigating dozens of timber sales in the region that propose to log in spotted owl habitat." And bumper stickers with messages such as DON'T LIKE LOGGING? TRY WIPING WITH A SPOTTED OWL and SPOTTED OWLS TASTE LIKE CHICKEN offer a glimpse at another side of the story.

Preserving rivers is on the K-S Wild agenda, as is restoring forests. The K-S Wild propaganda lists what it considers the leading threats to the rivers and forests, to the owls and the fish. Habitat is degraded by off-road vehicles. Overgrazing pollutes water and damages flora. Illegal mining ruins salmon spawning grounds. Excessive commercial logging on public lands hurts fragile forests.

As part of the K-S Wild strategy to combat these threats, the group proposed to the Interior Department that public land on the north side of the Klamath River up to the Oregon border be proclaimed a National Monument. As soon as word of the Monument proposal drifted down the river, the two camps squared off against each other: the "greenies" on one side, the settlers on the other. A parade of K-S WILD LIES and NO MONUMENT signs appeared along Highway 96. The tough talk I heard from settlers was matched on the other side by dedicated environmentalists like George Sexton, K-S Wild's conservation director.

Sexton and I meet at a brewery called Caldera along Ashland's Lithia Creek. He's brought his dog; he orders a pint. Man's best friend trips the waitress with its leash and she catches herself before landing

Environmentalist George Sexton worries Jefferson divisiveness could lead to violence.

face-first on the floor and, in a typical exercise of Oregon Nice, he checks on her well-being and apologizes to her for his mutt, just as she apologizes to him for her misstep and asks if the dog is okay.

While the waitress fetches the beer, we start talking about the conflicting interests and personalities flinging charges and counter-charges at each other in this isolated pocket of America. "I think that the degree of polarization and the degree of demonization in Siskiyou County is greater than in the country as a whole," Sexton tells me when I suggest that the divisiveness I'm finding in Jefferson is a metaphor for the political stalemates across America.

The menu at Caldera reflects the Ashland ethos. You can order a hamburger made of ground beef, but it's third on the list of burgers, after the garden burger (made with soy) and the black bean burger (served with cabbage and chipotle aioli). Other burger options include the salmon burger and the mahi mahi burger (the latter served with passion fruit aioli). Sexton is dressed in what I'm getting accustomed to as Oregon casual for plenty of business meetings: shorts, T-shirt, and a baseball cap. (Still influenced by a non-Jeffersonian business meeting ethos, I had stopped at the Medford Macy's because I forgot my "business casual" clothing at home in Eugene and had left the house for the drive south wearing a pair of scruffy jeans with a sloppy, un-ironed shirt. Now I'm decked out in that same deep blue cotton dress shirt and white linen slacks I wore when I met with Anthony Intiso and Liz Bowen.) Black plastic glasses frame Sexton's bright blue eyes, his beard is showing gray, and his ready smile lights up often to punctuate the tough talk.

"The rhetoric I see on the Internet and at the sheriff's events often has veiled and not so veiled at all references to violence." Sexton is quick to explain what he considers is a worrisome lack of civility outside of gentile Ashland over on the California side of the border. "There's a lot of talk of a coming civil war. There's a lot of talk of taking up arms. Not just the rhetoric. The imagery often involves gun holsters. Imagery that's been created against the Siskiyou Crest Monument proposal has things like mock hangings and effigies. I like to think that the majority of the political discourse in this country is not quite that extreme. There aren't a lot of moderating forces in Siskiyou County. It's still the Wild West in a lot of ways. The rhetoric and the intimidation are more extreme in Siskiyou County than you see in most other places regarding politics in general and natural resources issues in particular."

Sexton showed me examples. One is a photograph of a couple of scarecrow-like figures, one holding a pistol and the other a rifle, posed next to a faux grave marker that reads: HERE LIES KS WILD/1997-2011/THEY DIED TRYING TO TAKE THAT WHICH WAS NOT THEIRS. Others are comments posted to the K-S Wild website. Freetrapper2004 wrote, "I see a day in the near future that we will have to take up arms to protect our God given rights from leftist groups such as yours. I pray we will be able to stop you at the ballot box but if not then I pray for victory in the comming [sic] civil war that will commence once the people of this once free and great nation wake up and find that you leftist [sic] have taken steps to destroy our Constitution and Bill of Rights to further your tree hugger agenda. Be careful who you try to trample on, things are becoming serious!"

Another e-mail threatened arson. "I have lived in H.C. [Happy Camp] all my life and lately I have heard about two dozen people say that when this area becomes a monument they are all heading in different directions with two boxes of road flares each. So enjoy your charred monument. I hope you make the right decision and leave these people alone. Before all of this is just a memory!!!!!"

Michelle was another wishing K-S Wild the worst, writing, "You people have your head up your asses!!! You are very selfish people that don't desire to live!!!! You are very very wrong about the suction dredge and the lies you tell concerning dredging. I hope someone someday takes each and everyone [*sic*] of you enviros. Hey all you enviros should have a giant Earth Day party, so that you are in one place so that some nut can blow you animals away!!!!!"

From cowboy444 came this rant: "So, what do we have to do to reclaim OUR National Parks and all of the other areas claimed by UNESCO? I'm ready for armed conflict if necessary. KICK UN OUT OF THE US." Reno badboy added, "Time to start putting "GREENIES" in the cross hairs!!! Locked and loaded! Ready, aim, . . . " With a law degree—and specialized study in environmental and natural resources law from Lewis and Clark University, along with undergraduate work at Reed College—George Sexton is not some outside agitator, as Ronald Reagan used to call those of us Berkeley students protesting his policies when he was California governor and is reputed to have said, "When you've seen one redwood, you've seen them all." (According to the fact checkers at snopes.com, the "seen them all" comment came while the future president was campaigning for governor, and although it was not quite so glib it was just as thoughtless. In a San Francisco speech to the Western Wood Products Association in 1966—when debate over protecting redwoods in a National Park was fierce—Reagan said, "We've got to recognize that where the preservation of a natural resource like the redwoods is concerned, there is a common sense limit. I mean, if you've looked at a hundred thousand acres or so of trees—you know, a tree is a tree, how many more do you need to look at?"[102])

In fact Sexton's Pacific Northwest roots grow deep. He grew up in Oregon and learned to love the wilderness as he watched it being ravaged for timber. "I got to see the Mt. Hood National Forest creamed during the eighties. When I was knee high to a grasshopper my grandfather would take me to the Upper Clackamas and we would fish for trout. My grandfather drove a log truck and he told me about the evils of logging." The waitress interrupts and he orders another pint. "The Mt. Hood National Forest became a sea of clear-cuts," and Sexton became an environmental activist. "I am an Oregonian and I am a citizen of the State of Jefferson." He says it not defensively, but deliberately, and with a tone that implies a western saloon–like challenge of: Want to make something of it?

"The vitriol that is expressed towards the Karuk tribe I find particularly disturbing," Sexton says, vitriol he sees expressed on Internet exchanges between gold miners frustrated that their dredges are banned from the Klamath River. "They talk about finishing the job, in terms of genocide toward the Karuk tribe. There's a lot of joking about scalping and very unseemly stuff." It's much more "violence tinged and angry" than what he observes in the rest of the country, Sexton says again about Siskiyou County politics. Massive unemployment and the collapse of the fishing, mining, and timber industries helps explain local frustrations. "When you're struggling economically and you feel like you are in an isolated part of the state where Sacramento doesn't hear you, and certainly Washington, DC doesn't hear you, there's a tendency to really want someone to blame—to blame the 'other' and to demonize your opponents as worthy of having violence inflicted upon them."

It's a troubling analysis to listen to, especially in the privileged environment of Ashland with its elitist organic Caldera beer (only two dollars a pint; we're there at happy hour). The talk of violence in the congenial creekside tavern reminds me of the similar words—from another point of view—that I heard just days before in Seiad Valley where trailer park owner Bruce Johnson told me, "I think it's a lot closer to bloodshed than anybody in the city ever contemplates."

While George Sexton takes a breath and drinks some beer, I point out that opponents of his style of conservation speak about him and his work with the same sort of characterization that he uses for them—that environmentalists are out of control and are trying to ruin rural lifestyles. "Is there no common ground?" I ask. "Is there no room for compromise?" Sexton answers by listing what the adversaries share. "There's a common distrust in authoritarian government. There's a love of being outdoors. There's a common Jefferson heritage of do-it-yourself skills and being a part of the wilderness rather than looking at it through a TV screen." He says he tries to feel empathy for the "K-S Wild Lies" crowd.

"We've taken our foot off the gas pedal," he says about the National Monument proposal. Funny, he chooses a cliché derived from driving cars to describe the status of his efforts to carve a car-free zone out of the nearby forests. "Our intent was not to shove a Monument down underrepresented people's throats. Our intent was for federal lands on the Siskiyou Crest to have a more coherent management strategy." K-S Wild wildly underestimated the negative response to their proposed Monument, he says, and—to continue with the car comparison—their lobbying efforts for the Monument shifted into neutral. "Without a local group like us pushing really hard day and night for a Monument there is zero chance that it will occur." He draws out the "z" sound in zero, emphasizing it, saying the White House would not want to waste its political capital creating a Monument unpopular with many local residents. But even were the proposed Monument established along the Klamath, he points to the Cascade-Siskiyou National Monument, on the Oregon side of the border, as proof that the No Monument activists need not be paranoid. "No one had their land taken. No one lost their water rights. It all had to do with how you managed lands that were already federal lands."

"You could solve any coherent management crisis by creating Jefferson and letting the new state administer the public lands in question," I suggest.

"There you go," he laughs and takes a swig of his beer, and again turns serious. "Siskiyou County is not America. It is impossible to have a reasoned debate there. How you get ahead in Siskiyou County politics is by being more anti–Native American and more anti-environmental than the next guy." He sums up the prevailing attitudes he finds when he ventures there: "We're going to beat you up. You're an outsider. We hate you." K-S Wild, promoting its National Monument proposal, "has it easy compared with how the Karuk tribe has it or compared with how the Klamath River Keeper has it."

Again I think back to what Bruce Johnson told me about the Karuk tribe. "I'm tired of these sons-of-bitches," he said. "They've cost me a hundred thousand dollars because they're lying rat fuckers." Erica Terence grew up along the Klamath and is the executive director of the Klamath River Keeper working "against environmental injustices," as the organization describes her role. Liz Bowen describes that work differently on the Pie N Politics website, calling Terence's lament that the decimated coho population in the Klamath once numbered in the thousands a "huge lie."[103] "Every month they publish a hit piece on Erica Terence," says George Sexton, expressing concern about her health and safety. "It's in Liz's interests to hate K-S Wild, to hate the Klamath River Keeper, and to hate the Karuk tribe more than anyone else. That's what will get her attention and political cachet."

But Sexton says he refuses to return the emotion. "I don't hate Liz Bowen. I don't hate the Siskiyou County Tea Party Patriots. I don't even hate Marcia Armstrong." Marcia Armstrong is the Siskiyou County supervisor representing District 5, the Scott Valley. She writes a weekly column in the *Siskiyou Daily News* and asks her readers questions like: "Is the Endangered Species Act being used to protect true declining native species or to exert power and control over privately owned natural resources?" And: "What is the origin of the wolves coming into California that the federal government wants to protect as endangered?"

I pulled out my notebook and asked George Sexton the questions I noted while cruising Jefferson, questions that Liz Bowen and others wanted me to ask him. "Why do you want to ruin my life-style?" and "Why do you want to prevent me from earning a living?" and "Why do you want to destroy my business?"

Sexton takes another swig of beer. "I try to have empathy for those feelings," he says, especially since he's sure that even without environmentalists like him on the scene, old growth logging would have stopped at some point in the Klamath National Forest. "The last thing I want to do is destroy anyone's livelihood or business." He is convinced that Happy Camp and Seiad Valley could be prosperous communities in balance with the natural resources that support them, and that models exist to prove it. "The people who are saying either we must eliminate the coho salmon and prevent wolves from ever returning and log the old growth and retain the dams or you hate us and you want us to be jobless offer a false choice. You can't just clear-cut your way to prosperity."

"But the other side tells me that's not what they want. I hear essentially what you say. 'I love the wilderness,' but then they add, 'and we can operate a sustainable forest products industry.'"

No they can't, is his reply. "You look at what the Siskiyou County Board of Supervisors actually proposes—the federal forest management proposal that's on their website—and it's the furthest thing that you can imagine from sustainability. And the sheriff says closing even one mile of road in the forest is somehow an abrogation of the Constitution."

Suction dredging is next on my list of questions from those opposed to the Monument. "Where's the science?" say the miners. "There's no science that proves suction dredging harms the river."

Nonsense, says Sexton. He cites a 1999 Forest Service study that determined the dredging creates attractive beds for coho that coho should not be using. "There is peer-reviewed science that says tailings that suction dredging produce are attractive to salmon and steelhead as spawning redds. Once salmon and steelhead use the tailings as spawning redds—since they are not anchored the way a natural riverbed would be anchored—when winter high floods come through, the redds get blasted."

That leads to another question. "Why protect the coho, they are not a native species, they were introduced into the Klamath?"

I need more beer, is what I figure Sexton is thinking by the look on his face when I repeat the claim from the settlers I talked with along the Klamath who call coho an invasive species. Instead he sighs and restricts himself to a quiet, "Yeah, and then you take off the tin foil hat. Coho have been here for tens of thousands of years."

Next point: "Dredgers help clean the river by removing mercury."

Sexton points out that it was miners back in the nineteenth century who introduced mercury into the waterways. "The mercury was largely settled in the creeks because the mercury was produced so long ago." The dredging stirs up that settled mercury. Miners are able to collect and remove some of it. "The study that led to the moratorium in California indicated that it was likely that dredging reintroduced more mercury into the water stream than it removed."

Sexton dismisses all the miners' complaints as inconsequential in the face of what K-S Wild and the Karuk tribe are trying to accomplish together. "What I'm interested in, and what I think most conservationists and the tribes are interested in, is keeping coho from going extinct. What we're talking about is whether public rivers in public forests are worth more for salmon production for all or gold production for a few."

Nonetheless he appreciates the deep-seated frustrations and resentments roiling Jefferson blue-collar laborers. "If you've been working in the mill for twenty years and then you lose your job because of a damned owl, you're wondering why did this happen and why aren't people helping?" But there is a living to be made along the Klamath River, he is convinced, and history proves it. "Who has figured out how to make a living along the Klamath

River for the last ten thousand years? Well, it's not Liz Bowen and it's not Marcia Armstrong. It's the Karuk tribe." Sexton supports Karuk proposals to protect the forests from devastating wildfires with controlled burns, harvesting of small trees, and thinning underbrush. Wildfires devastate the salmon spawning grounds with silt from burned mountainsides.

The fire that I had been watching as its flames headed toward Seiad Valley finally was contained by the time Sexton and I met, but not until it burned almost twenty-four thousand acres. Instead of trying to extinguish the blaze, Sexton says the Forest Service should have protected homes, livestock, and businesses along the river and "let the back country burn. End this constant Forest Service circus of dumping millions of dollars and young people's lives into the back country suppressing fires in a fire dependent ecosystem."

There's no viable alternative to coho for the Happy Camp and Seiad Valley communities, Sexton is convinced. And there's no question in his mind that the settlers cannot turn back the clock to what they may consider were the good old days. "Is having signs on the entrance to towns saying, 'Environmentalists and city people and federal employees and wolves get the fuck out,' going to draw people there? Is that going to draw young families there? Is that going to draw tourists there? Is that going to draw new businesses there? I tend to think not." He orders a third pint and reiterates that he considers himself a Jeffersonian.

"The State of Jefferson means feeling like you're connected to this place, feeling like you're connected to your neighbors, and feeling like you're going to work to leave your neighbors and the place better than you found." Sounds like a litany worthy of translation into Latin as a motto on the Jefferson state seal.

Chapter Thirty-Two

THE ART OF JEFFERSON

WHEN HE WAS DIRECTOR OF THE SCHNEIDER MUSEUM OF ART AT Southern Oregon University in Ashland, Michael Crane was inspired by remnants of the secession movement that he kept discovering in and around his new Oregon home. He decided to curate a show for the museum with works, as his call announced, "about the Mythical State of Jefferson." He sought entries from artists, writers, actors, musicians, dancers, and designers. "We want to know," the museum asked the arts community, "if you have something to say about democracy in America? We want to know what you think or feel about taking destiny in your own hands? We want to hear from you about whether creating another state would be a good idea. In addition, we want to know if you have a new (or old) perspective about the State of Jefferson to share with audiences?"

There was no shortage of submissions, but curator Crane was not just looking for pretty pictures. "I got a lot of landscapes," he told me shortly after the exhibition finished its successful run at the museum. "People wanted me to show what it looks like. I wanted to show what Jefferson feels like."

One of his favorites of over sixty pieces on display was the work of Portland artist Erik Steen, who makes beer in addition to art. "His theory is that beer has always been the drink of revolutions. Not wine. It's beer." Steen brewed ninety-nine bottles of beer for the opening of the exhibit as a salute to Highway 99, the route into Yreka blocked by the 1941 Jeffersonians.

A reproduction of the Proclamation of Independence was on display as were the (staged?) photographs of the secessionists blocking Highway 99.

The mythical moved to the virtual with an installation created by Ethan Ham and Ethan Miller. They placed a wireless router (topped with a miniature Jefferson double cross flag) in the gallery, a router that was programmed to connect passing laptops and smartphones to the Internet. Whenever a passerby would search the web for a site that included an address within Jefferson's boundaries, the device substituted "Jefferson" for "Oregon" or "California." Click on Ashland Chamber of Commerce for directions to their office, for example, and up popped 110 East Main Street, Ashland, Jefferson. Because of our ubiquitous use of the web, we've become conditioned (too often) to accept what we find via the Internet as fact. Just seeing Ashland, Jefferson, on the screen created a new reality to the movement. Ham explained that the piece, which the artists called "The Virtual State of Jefferson," "explores how the Internet has become one of our primary windows for viewing the world and how the realities it presents can be authoritative, fictive, self-deluding, and enlightening."

"The artist community loved the show," according to curator Crane, because artists tend to embrace the Jeffersonian "independent, take-your-destiny-into-your-own-hands kind of spirit." Crane fancies himself a Jeffersonian, with or without any real possibility of a 51st state. "I think that even positing it is an expression of our form of democracy, that is fantastic." He subscribes to the idea that freedom in America is expressed by the opportunity to create community, and he believes the arts should instruct politically, spiritually, and socially. "Can art have an impact?" he asks rhetorically. "Can it create change? What are the different aesthetic strategies we employ to persuade?" He sees Jefferson as a "wonderful expression."

Art should instigate dialogue, Michael Crane tells me. He dreams that art could help bring the divergent interests in Jefferson together. "Maybe that's too idealistic," he wonders aloud, but he's smiling, convinced of the mitigating and mediating roles art should play, and he offers up Stanton Delaplane's 1941 dispatches as an unexpected example.

"I understand that it was Delaplane who penned the Proclamation of Independence," he says. "He wrote it."

"Art as news," I suggest about the charge that Delaplane crossed a journalistic line from observer to behind-the-scenes participant.

"Art as news," he agrees, and adds another charge. The woman in one of the famous photographs of cars being stopped by Jefferson border guards was a friend of Delaplane's.

"Staged?" I ask about the notorious, widely circulated image.

"Staged," says Crane.

"Art," I offer.

"Exactly! Exactly!" He's enthusiastic.

"Art made as a photograph shot in the field."

"Exactly." Michael Crane loves the blurring of what was presented as journalism and what may have been created as art.

Chapter Thirty-Three

At the HempFest and with the State of Jefferson Band

It's a sparkling mid-summer day when Sheila and I turn off the main road from Cave Junction to the Oregon Caves National Monument and head toward the parking lot of the Jefferson State Music Festival and Hemp Expo. over forty bands! yells the flyer and onsite camping! Promised is valuable information at the Hemposium, seminars with talks on how to grow indoors and on how to grow outdoors. The Hemposium kicks off with the all-important "Know and Protect Your Rights" session. The band that named itself State of Jefferson is on the bill.

The neo-hippie directing traffic points us toward a place to park.

"Boy, is it ever hot today," I say, making conversation.

He agrees and points to his bright red, sunburned forehead.

"Hey," I reprimand him. "Where's your hat? You should be wearing a hat!"

"Yeah," he agrees, "and I should have gone to college. Does that answer it?" He laughs what I take to be a marijuana-influenced laugh and waves me on to park. My newish old Volvo feels out of place. If only we still had our 1976 VW bus (named Many Payments by Sheila), with the eight-track player in the dash and the bed in the back, with our friend Buckeye's painting of a cow skull decorating the spare tire cover, and an america love it or leave it sticker on the rear bumper for ironic relief.

A happy Jefferson State HempFest native.

We park and wander around looking at the tie-dye and smelling the sweet smell of the dope in question, along with the aroma of another sixties-era reminder. "I didn't like patchouli then," Sheila sniffs, "and I still don't like it." Reggae blasts from one of the bandstands. Flags festooned with marijuana leaves flap. I spot a booth selling State of Jefferson T-shirts, shirts that show off the now-familiar double cross.

"Tell me about Jefferson," I ask the vendor.

"It actually almost happened," he says about 51st statehood. "I'm not sure of the date. They were about to sign the papers. It was based on the tax dollars."

"What papers?" I ask.

"I hope I get this right." He's a friendly fellow; Ryan Casad of Eugene introduces himself. "I feel like I should bust out the Wikipedia page."

A contemporary Jefferson artifact.

"What papers were they about to sign?" I ask again. I find it intriguing that he's at an event headlined State of Jefferson and that he's selling State of Jefferson paraphernalia but that he doesn't seem to know much about the place. He laughs. "I guess I should have paid more attention in school." But he puts my question into appropriate perspective. "I am at the HempFest, you know."

So he is.

The band that calls itself State of Jefferson was scheduled to play later that day. Much later. But it was too windy and hot to sit around and wait hours to talk with the bandmates. Besides, their attention understandably would be directed on their performance, not on my questions about Jefferson and the relationship of their music to the place. Sheila and I waved good-bye to the HempFest and meandered back to Ashland.

"Jefferson is a culture," Joe Ginet tells me. I'm sitting with him and two other members of the State of Jefferson band at Creekside Pizza in Ashland, along with the first pitcher of beer for the evening. These local musicians didn't just name their band after their adopted state; they embrace their own Jeffersonian philosophy. Joe's stage name, for example, is Joe Jefferson. "We're Oregonians, but we don't live in Salem or Eugene or Portland. Down in Eureka or Siskiyou County, they're Californians, but they really don't remind me of people from Venice Beach that much. They remind me more of people from Ashland." Ginet's massive dreadlocks are mostly stuffed deep into a gray knit cap. His brown beard meets his chest. He speaks rapidly and his face seems permanently affixed with a warm, gentle smile. "There is an off the grid mentality that is pretty prevalent in rural Jefferson," he says, in an attempt to explain what unites the disparate types who call Jefferson their home. Ginet starts to list the Jefferson subcultures. He identifies homesteaders' descendants and Native Americans. He adds what he calls "East Coast, trust fund, bar mitzvah money kids who ended up here after a good trip." Jeffersonian differences, he says, tend to dissolve around common Wild West attitudes, a lifestyle that he sums up by paraphrasing his neighbors: "I'll live at the end of a gravel road and cut my own firewood in a house with no permits."

Joe Ginet sings with the band. He plays guitar and mandolin, along with harmonica. Differences of opinions that divide Jeffersonians, he says, tend to dissipate in the face of pragmatic concerns. Conflict is a luxury you can afford when daily needs don't require you live in what the musician refers to as harmony. "When you're sharing a nine-mile dirt driveway with your redneck neighbor and you're a hippie, guess what? If you're both going to be there for life, you're going to find common ground. You're going to get along. You're going to pull his truck out of the snow and he's going to help you fix your chain saw. I know so many rednecks who slip out to smoke a joint with their hippie neighbor. That's how it works." Another smile. "There is that cross pollination." More beer.

The band tells the same story in the lyrics of one of their signature tunes, a rollicking bluegrass anthem. "Jefferson," no surprise, is the title. "Jefferson, Jefferson," demands the refrain, "leave us to ourselves."

Ryan Redding's is one of the voices singing "Leave us to ourselves," and he plays bass with the band. His long curly brown locks are kept out of his face by his black baseball cap emblazoned with red stitching that spells out STATE OF JEFFERSON. His grin also comes easily as he talks about his home state. "That's something we've focused on," he says about the band's commitment to harmony—in their music and throughout their state. "We're inspired to create this community that is us all working together." Growing up in rural Jefferson, he says, the band witnessed the differences and issues that divided people. A goal of their music making is to build a diverse audience that bridges Jefferson's subcultures. "Our album has a picture of the world on it. That's because you can be a State of Jefferson–conscious person—being here together as one— whether it's a geographical location or not." His Jefferson is not just place, he says, once the concept of Jefferson is internalized. "All it is," he offers with a beatific smile, "is a feeling of love— whether I'm in the physical State of Jefferson, the emotional State of Jefferson, or the spiritual State of Jefferson."

The band's organist is another singer, Erik Vestnys. His red hair is tied back tight and he's wearing a green T-shirt festooned with a towering conifer. "During the seventy years from its latest incarnation," he says, referring to the 1941 statehood episodes, "there have been many conflicts between the different types who live in the State of Jefferson. I think coming into the new century, people are learning how to live together within their own communities. We see it firsthand, living in the rural parts of the State of Jefferson." After

The boys in the (Jefferson) band: (from left to right) Ryan Redding, Joe (Jefferson) Ginet, and Erik Vestnys.

all the divisiveness I've been exposed to researching Jefferson, it is a relief to listen to the optimism. It's optimism tempered with realism. "In the urban areas," Vestnys accepts, "you are dealing with a lot more conflict because you have a limited amount of space and a limited amount of resources." But at home in the countryside, he experiences growing cooperation between Jeffersonians learning "to live somewhat in harmony with your neighbors, whether or not they have the same belief systems as you."

But the band is not unaware of the fights playing out in pockets of Jefferson far from their bucolic Applegate Valley along the Rogue River on the back road from Grants Pass to Ashland. Erik Vestnys cites an example from the sector of Jefferson along the Klamath River on the California side of the border, "There you have a sustained native population, and here you have an extinct native population."

An official State of Jefferson highway marker.

"It's not as diverse as Brooklyn," admits Joe Ginet about Jefferson, but he knows that "there are a lot of different people here." His example is Frankie Hernandez, a fellow musician featured on an album produced by the band, a compilation that showcases local Jefferson talent. "Frankie is of Mexican descent from Austin, Texas. He's chosen to call Ashland his home and that's where he makes his music." Mariachi-like trumpets introduce Frankie Hernandez on the sampler CD. His tune is titled "Puff One Down," and is an ode to one of Jefferson's cash crops. "Puff one down for the convict," he sings, "puff in the face of the cynic. Puff one down for the grandma who went to the wrong side of town for her medic."

There is beauty in Jefferson's diversity, Ginet believes. "We can try to pigeonhole groups all day, but ultimately they're all here for the same reason—there's a goodness in this area."

Another pitcher of beer arrives at the table and Ryan Redding starts to recount his version of Jefferson's 1941 rise and fall. The new state was established, he insists, and the war did not change that fact.

"What they did in 1941 had no legal ramifications," I protest. "Some guys anointed another guy governor. Then they proclaimed themselves a state."

"But it was signed into law by the president at the time," Redding protests.

"No!" I complain.

"It was," Redding insists.

Robert Gable searches his father's Jefferson archives as his mother keeps watch. Despite Ryan Redding's faith, there's no Jefferson statehood law signed by President Roosevelt in these or any other collections of Jefferson memorabilia. Belief in that ethereal document is yet another intriguing element in the never-ending legend of the elusive state of Jefferson.

"No," I repeat.

"It was," Redding says again. "By Roosevelt. He granted them statehood. It was going to be released in the San Francisco newspaper the next day and Pearl Harbor happened."

"No," I say again, and I'm shaking my head, offering a quickie version of the 1941 Jefferson antics. "Where do you get your information?" I ask Redding, who remains true to his version of Jeffersonian lore.

All three of the band members are smiling at my attention to historical details. Joe Ginet laughs and answers my query. "He gets his information from the hills! There's some serious folklore out there." Erik Vestnys adds, "It's the mythical State of Jefferson!"

We're drinking a tasty Jefferson beer brewed a few miles up I-5 in Central Point called Workers Pale Ale, and it's time for another round.

EPILOGUE

"I WANT TO BE ALONE," SAID GRETA GARBO, PLAYING GRUSINSKAYA in the film *Grand Hotel* back in 1932.

Since it is unclear whether Jefferson backers choose to name their new state after Jefferson Davis or Thomas Jefferson, I propose the secessionists consider reinvigorating their cause with a name change. Jefferson—despite the marvelous works of Thomas Jefferson and the lasting attractiveness for some of Jefferson Davis's Confederacy—is somewhat mundane for a state name, especially a new state. We already show off the legacy of a founding father with George's namesake, Washington State (not to mention that federal protectorate, Washington, DC). There is a state named after a businessman, Pennsylvania. There are states named for the Crown we overthrew, like the Carolinas (Latin for Charles, in honor of King Charles I). The Spanish heritage in the Southwest left us with descriptive state names such as Nevada (snow) and Colorado (red). The French gave us Louisiana (more legacy of royalty). Several states are named after vanquished Indians, from Tennessee to Utah and beyond. Jefferson disappears in this milieu as just another typical state name.

I propose the Jeffersonians jettison Jefferson and call their place in the sun (and—maybe more often—the rain), Garbo. She is famous for wanting to be left alone. They want to be left alone, or so they say. They want to invent a new state. Greta Gustafsson invented her name: Greta Garbo. Or director Mauritz Stiller invented it. The origin is unclear, just as is the origin of the state names Oregon and California.

Garbo. It has a nice look and ring to it. The typography is appealing when it is attached to place names, as is the sound when the new state name is spoken in conjunction with its major cities. Klamath Falls, Garbo. Yreka, Garbo. Port Orford, Garbo. Add the zip code and it looks official: Ashland, Garbo 97520. Eureka, Garbo!

Garbo: enigmatic and private with a wry nod to celebrity. For a place where history—in fact and fancy—was created by the deft use of publicity, the name change to Garbo would put the former Jefferson (look how bland Jefferson already looks compared with Garbo!) in headlines around the world.

Garbo, an ideal name for a place that claims it just wants to be left alone.

Acknowledgments

Greta Garbo may well have wanted to be alone, but were I left alone, this study of the State of Jefferson would not exist.

A hearty western, "Thanks, partner-honey," to the first editor of my work: my wife, Sheila Swan Laufer—her sharp red pencil protects me from myself. The tenacious research skills of my colleague at the University of Oregon School of Journalism and Communication, graduate teaching fellow Charles Deitz, helped me uncover fascinating Jefferson history from critical primary sources, including Jefferson citizens who made (and continue to make) that history.

When one of those sources, Robert Gable, the son of Port Orford's Mayor Gilbert Gable, showed me examples of his father's 1941 official correspondence, I handled a letter from Oregon governor Charles A. Sprague with particular appreciation, holding the paper up to the light ("Neenah Old Council Tree Bond 100% Rag Content," read the watermark on the official state letterhead), feeling the heft of the paper and enjoying the look of the inked impressions made by the governor's typist (identified simply as "B" at the bottom of the letter with the code abandoned in this e-mail era: CAS:B). No hard drive crash could do to the governor's seventy-two-year-old correspondence what my MacBook did to me when it crashed as I was completing the book, taking with it to Apple Hell both text and images. Another crucial colleague at the university, the J-School's ubiquitous IT coordinator Andre Chinn, worked with data recovery experts to salvage the critical files. And Chinn's crew in the IT office provided needed technical support throughout the project, always with smiles, often with jokes: Tom Lundberg, Ryan Stasel, Matt Schmidt, Ashley Campbell, Cameron Shultz, Sharwin Karande, Qian Wu, and Ariana Whitty.

Librarians throughout Jefferson curate records, memorabilia, and artifacts relating to the incipient statehood movement. Especially helpful were Midge Hayes at the Port Orford Library and Marsha Eblen at the College of the Siskiyous Library in Weed, where Dennis Freeman maintains the special collections and a fat Jefferson file. My friend Tom Corwin graciously spent time in the stacks of the library in Mill Valley, California, to locate an important and nearly forgotten Stanton Delaplane interview. Kirsten Baldock, in the Magazines and Newspapers Department of the Oakland Public Library, located a needed *Oakland Tribune* article based on an incomplete clip. Her clues were a wrong date, an incomplete headline and an adjacent display ad for the October sale at Brent's promising pots and pans at a bargain price "for a limited time only." The Yreka community television station KYCT is a repository of raw newsreel footage of the 1941 antics, along with interviews made years later with participants of those famous days.

A tip of the hat to my partners on our southern California radio border project— "Calexico: Bordering on a State of Mind"—Markos Kounalakis, Jim McKee, and Ryan Anderson. Our work together on the California-Mexican border stimulated my interest in what was happening at the other end of our state. And my friend Terry Phillips, another student of borders and fresh from making history himself running for Congress, was a critical reader of early drafts of the manuscript. It was Phillips who authenticated the Greta Garbo quote from his lonesome redoubt in Bakersfield: "I want to be alone."

When I suggested that the tales of Jefferson cried out for a book, my Globe Pequot editor Erin Turner became an immediate champion of the project. Hardly a surprise that she would relate to rural secessionists considering that she established her office out west in

Helena, Montana—2,359.1 Google miles from company headquarters back east in Connecticut.

After exploring the wilds of Jefferson and meeting scores of Jeffersonians, I'm convinced that the alienation many of them feel from the rest of the world, along with the schisms that often separate them like the Hatfields and McCoys, offer lessons for us all. So I thank the characters who shared their Jefferson with me for this study. Not only can we all learn from them, they prove to be a pretty entertaining bunch of renegades.

Notes

1   www.pbs.org/wnet/need-to-know/the-daily-need/splitting-california-in-two/10504/.

2   Medina, Jennifer, "California Counties Talk of Cutting Ties to State," *New York Times*, July 13, 2011, p. A17.

3   "Members of Town Chamber of Commerce Attempt Secessionist Movement from Colorado to New Mexico," *Denver Post Empire* magazine, June 3, 1973, p. 55.

4   http://explorepahistory.com/story.php?storyId=1-9-11&chapter=4.

5   Mayo, Michael, "Is It Time for South Florida to Break Away from Tallahassee?", (Ft. Lauderdale) *Sun Sentinel*, May 14, 2011.

6   "Two GOP Legislators Propose Separating Cook County from Illinois," (Springfield) *State Journal-Register*, November 23, 2011.

7   McCormick, Peter J., "The 1992 Secession Movement in Southwest Kansas," *Great Plains Quarterly*, January 1, 1995, pp. 247–58.

8   "Eastern Shore Secession Move Inevitable," *Salisbury* (MD) *News*, October 14, 2010.

9   Di Leo, Michael and Smith, Eleanor, *Two Californias: The Truth about the Split-State Movement*, Island Press (Covelo, CA), 1983, p. 165.

10   Delaplane, Stanton, "Secession Land's Publicity Man: 'This is the Promised Land of Broken Promises,'" *San Francisco Chronicle*, November 30, 1941.

11 Thomas Van Pelt letter to John K. Lamerick, July 15, 1856, Cayuse, Yakima and Rogue River Wars Papers, Bx 047, Special Collections & University Archives, University of Oregon Libraries, Eugene, Oregon.

12 Kristof, Nicholas D., "Nobuo Fujita, 85, Is Dead; Only Foe to Bomb America," *New York Times*, October 3, 1997.

13 www.clr.pdx.edu/projects/lakes/garrison.php.

14 "Mayor Gilbert Gable Dies Suddenly Here," *Port Orford Post*, December 5, 1941, p. 1.

15 Delaplane, Stanton, "Mayor Gable, 49th State Leader, Dies," *San Francisco Chronicle*, December 3, 1941.

16 www.weather.com/outlook/travel/vacationplanner/compare/results?from=vac_compare&clocid1=USCA0183&clocid2=USOR0274.

17 Rheinhardt, Richard, "The Short, Happy History of the State of Jefferson," *The American West*, May 1972, p. 41.

18 *Oakland Tribune*, October 14, 1941.

19 "Curry Beware," *Oregonian*, October 4, 1941.

20 Ludlow, Lynn, "The Ever-amazing Ding-Dong Daddy of the D Car Line," *San Francisco Examiner*, January 5, 1981, p. A16.

21 Gorney, Cynthia, "The State of the American Newspaper: Battle of the Bay," *American Journalism Review*, January-February 1999.

22 www.lib.berkeley.edu/give/bene61/bene61story5.html.

23 Fimrite, Peter, "CA Grizzly Bear Monarch: A Symbol of Suffering," *San Francisco Chronicle*, May 3, 2011.

24 www.library.ca.gov/history/symbols.html#Heading4.

25 *Siskiyou Daily News*, December 1, 1941.

26 Davis, W. N., Jr., "State of Jefferson," *California Historical Quarterly*, June 1952, pp. 125–38. *Note:* I rely on former California state historian W. N. Davis Jr. for the day-by-day timeline of events leading up to the proclamation of Jefferson statehood in Yreka.

27 Wilson, Steve, "Jefferson State of Mind," *American History*, February 2005, Volume 39, Issue 6.

28 *Siskiyou Daily News*, December 1 and 2, 1941.

29 Oregon's Curry County, along with Siskiyou, Del Norte, Lassen, and Trinity Counties in California, made up the 1941 version of Jefferson.

30 Rock, James T., "'State of Jefferson' Vision Hangs On," *California Historian*, Spring 1998.

31 Delaplane, Stanton, "If They Want Copper They Can Come Up and Dig for It!", *San Francisco Chronicle*, November 28, 1941, p. 7.

32 Davies, Lawrence K., "'Seceders' Block California Roads/ Miners With Pistols Halt Autoists and Give Out Handbills on '49th' State/Sales Tax Paying Barred/Residents of 'Jefferson' Intent on Advertising Mineral Wealth and Need for Roads," *New York Times*, November 28, 1941, p. 25.

33 Nolte, Carl, "Independence Is a State of Mind on California's Frontier," *San Francisco Chronicle*, June 3, 2001.

34 Stone, Robert D., "Dunsmuir Youths Punctured Yreka's Capitol Dream," *Dunsmuir Centennial Book*, Dunsmuir Centennial Committee, 1985.

35 Medina, Jennifer, "California Counties Talk of Cutting Ties to State," *New York Times*, July 13, 2011, p. A18.

36 *San Francisco Chronicle*, December 9, 1941.

37 Davis, W. N., Jr., "State of Jefferson," *California Historical Quarterly*, June 1952, p. 135.

38 Kumar, Sheila V., Associated Press dispatch, October 10, 2011.

39 Winkler, Adam, "The History of Guns," *Atlantic* magazine, September 2011.

40 McManis, Sam, "Next Exit: Weed Makes Hay with Its Name," *Sacramento Bee*, October 20, 2011, p. 1D.

41   Murphy, Gerald P., "The State of Jefferson," *KSOR Guide to the Arts*, July 1991.

42   www.siskiyouhistory.org/1875.html.

43   Paterson, T. W., "Alex: The 'Other' Dunsmuir Son Is Little Remembered in Tributes," *Cowichan Valley Citizen*, October 22, 2010.

44   Evans, Jim, "The 'Upstate California' Campaign Is Déjà Vu All Over Again for Stan Statham," *Sacramento News & Review*, January 3, 2002.

45   Kushman, Rick, "Assembly Backs Vote on Splitting State," *Sacramento Bee*, June 11, 1993.

46   http://portal.delaware.gov/facts/history/delhist.shtml.

47   http://www.sec.state.vt.us/kids/RevolutionRightsRules.pdf.

48   http://csumc.wisc.edu/wtlc/?q=node/72.

49   Walsh-Sarnecki, Peggy, "51st State? Yoopers Are Talking Up Secession from Michigan Again," *Detroit Free Press*, May 6, 2012.

50   www.washington.edu/uwired/outreach/cspn/Website/Classroom%20Materials/Reading%20the%20Region/Aggressive%20Regionalism/Commentary/17.html.

51   http://cascadia-institute.org/name.html.

52   http://columbia.washingtonhistory.org/anthology/earliestsettlers/tradeAndChange.aspx.

53   http://memory.loc.gov/cgi-bin/ampage?collId=mtj1&fileName=mtj1page046.db&recNum=1321.

54   Dolan, Maura, "9th Circuit Overturns Suction Dredge Gold Mining Rulings," *Los Angeles Times*, June 2, 2012.

55   www.dfg.ca.gov/suctiondredge/.

56   Freeman, Mark, "Coho Habitat Subject of Lawsuit by Coalition of Environmental Organizations," *Ashland Daily Tidings*, October 26, 2012.

57 Yardley, William, "Tea Party Blocks Pact to Restore a West Coast River," *New York Times*, July 18, 2012.

58 www.doi.gov/news/pressreleases/2010_02_18_release.cfm.

59 Yardley, William, "Pact to Restore West Coast River, Negotiated in 2010, Is Blocked by Tea Party," *New York Times*, July 19, 2012, p. A18.

60 Martinez, Dave, "Scarecrow Row and Fall Festival Revives Downtown," *Herald and News*, October 28, 2012, p. A2.

61 Miller, Steve, "Examining the Economic Health of Our Region and Inviting Opinions on Its Likelihood to Get Better," *Herald and News*, October 27, 2012, p. A6.

62 www.vote2012tom.com/positions.

63 Brown, Richard D., *Strength of a People: The Idea of an Informed Citizenry in America, 1650–1870*, University of North Carolina Press, 1996, p. 89.

64 www.vote2012tom.com/positions.

65 http://envs.uoregon.edu/reference/aboutenvs/.

66 Most, Stephen, *River of Renewal: Myth & History in the Klamath Basin*, University of Washington Press, Seattle, 2006, p. xxxi.

67 Henderson, Bonnie, "Watershed Moment," *Oregon Quarterly*, Autumn 2012, p. 30.

68 Becker, Jo and Gellman, Barton, "Leaving No Tracks," *Washington Post*, July 27, 2007, p. A1.

69 Most, *River of Renewal*, p. 131.

70 www.klamathbucketbrigade.org/.

71 www.klamathbucketbrigade.org/green_fascism_how_ecologica_extremists_seek_to_curtai_freedom.htm.

72 *Guide to the Oregon Applegate Trail*, Friends of the Greensprings, Ashland, OR.

73 www.oregonencyclopedia.org/entry/view/boyle_
john_1887_1979/.

74 Lehman, Chris, "Clock Ticking for Klamath Dams," Oregon
Public Broadcasting News, February 3, 2010.

75 www.oregonlive.com/century/1970_intro.html.

76 Levstik, Frank R., "Jefferson Columbus Davis," *Encyclopedia of the
American Civil War*, Heidler, David S. and Jeanne T. Heidler,
eds., W.W. Norton & Company, New York, 2000, p. 572.

77 "Gen. Jefferson C. Davis Dead," *New York Times*, December
2, 1879. Reading the Davis obituary in the 1879 *Times* is a
reminder of attitudes that prevailed in that era. "General
Davis took command of the forces employed against the
Indians," wrote the anonymous *Times* scribe about the
Modoc Wars, "and forced the savages to surrender."

78 Rock, James, "'State of Jefferson' Vision Hangs On," *California
Historian*, Spring 1998.

79 Sanders, Garth, Jr., "State of Jefferson Would Not Coddle Its
Criminals," *Redding Record-Searchlight*, November 26, 1971.

80 Kepple, Todd, "The 'State of Jefferson' a Myth or a Real State
of Mind?" *Herald and News* (Klamath Falls, OR), March 26,
2000.

81 Fagan, Kevin, "'Jefferson' Feels Need to Secede," *San Francisco
Chronicle*, October 5, 2008, p. A1.

82 www.un.org/esa/dsd/agenda21/res_agenda21_01.shtml.

83 www.nationalatlas.gov/articles/government/a_national
parks.html.

84 www.theodoreroosevelt.org/life/conNatMonument.htm.

85 www.nps.gov/history/local-law/anti1906.htm.

86 www.blm.gov/or/resources/recreation/csnm/.

87 www.winnememwintu.us/who-we-are/.

88 www.winnememwintu.us/mccloud-salmon-restoration/.

89 http://stateofjeffersonpodcast.com/?page_id=31.

90 Kepple, "The 'State of Jefferson' a Myth or a Real State of Mind?"

91 "New State of Siskiyou," *Medford Mail*, December 2, 1909.

92 Sutton, Jack, *The Mythical State of Jefferson*, Josephine County Historical Society, 1965, p. 56.

93 *Ibid.*

94 Watson, Stu, "Jefferson State Never Succeeded," *Mail Tribune* (Medford, OR), March 23, 1989, p. 3C.

95 www.tshaonline.org/handbook/online/articles/vbk01.

96 Beckham, Stephen Dow, *Requiem for a People: The Rogue Indians and the Frontiersmen*, University of Oklahoma Press, Norman, 1971, p. 121.

97 www.ijpr.org/Feature.asp?FeatureID=1758.

98 "Site of Huge 1855 Indian Battle Found," *The Register-Guard* (Eugene, OR), September 27, 2012, p. B3.

99 www.oregonencyclopedia.org/entry/view/council_of_table_rock/.

100 Allen, Cain, "General Joseph Lane," Oregon Historical Society catalog number OrHi 1703, 2003.

101 Beckham, *Requiem for a People,* p. 124.

102 www.snopes.com/quotes/reagan/redwoods.asp.

103 http://pienpolitics.com/?p=8821.

Index

About the Author

Peter Laufer, PhD, is the author of more than a dozen books that deal with social and political issues, including *Mission Rejected: U.S. Soldiers Who Say No to Iraq, Wetback Nation: The Case for Opening the Mexican-American Border*, and a trilogy that interrogates the relationships of humans to other animals: *The Dangerous World of Butterflies, Forbidden Creatures*, and *No Animals Were Harmed*. He is the James Wallace Chair Professor in Journalism at the University of Oregon School of Journalism and Communication. More about his books, documentary films, and broadcasts, which have won the George Polk, Robert F. Kennedy, Edward R. Murrow and other awards, can be found at peterlaufer.com.